Wilson Meikuaya and Jackson Ntirkana
with Susan McClelland

THE LAST MAASAI WARRIORS

an autobiography

me to we
Better choices for a better world

Me to We
225 Carlton Street
Toronto ON Canada M5A 2L2
www.metowe.com/books

Distributed by
Greystone Books, D&M Publishers Inc.

Cataloguing in Publication data available
from Library and Archives Canada
ISBN: 978-1-927435-00-7 (pbk.)
ISBN: 978-1-927435-01-4 (ebook)

******

Cover and text design by Erin Aubrey
Art direction by Ryan Bolton and Erin Aubrey
Cover photographs by V. Tony Hauser
Printed and bound in Canada by Friesens
Text printed on 100% post-consumer, acid-free paper
Distributed in the U.S. by Publishers Group West

MIX
Paper from
responsible sources
FSC
www.fsc.org   FSC® C016245

THE LAST MAASAI WARRIORS

an autobiography

I would like to dedicate this book to my parents, Kerempe and Rureto Meikuaya, all of my brothers and sisters, and my entire community of Maji Moto. —Wilson Meikuaya

I would like to dedicate this book to my parents, Arami and Koimeren Ntrikana, all of my brothers and sisters, and my entire community of Naikarra. —Jackson Ntirkana

Contents

Foreword

by Craig and Marc Kielburger

The world is full of heroes.

After all, we live in a Hollywood culture that glamorizes and idolises strong, brave warriors who overcome incredible odds to save the day. These are, of course, most often merely fictional action-figures—characters with otherworldly powers from comic books and million-dollar blockbuster movies.

But thankfully there are true warriors among us who struggle every day to improve the lot of their families and communities. They are real-life heroes who must overcome real odds, and with a great deal at stake—like the survival of their people.

Meet Wilson Meikuaya and Jackson Ntirkana: warriors, tribesmen, leaders and friends from the Maasai Mara in East Africa. Theirs is an intensely rich culture that, despite a long and storied history of warring, invariably seeks peaceful means as the solution in a great many matters. It's also a culture founded on the supreme importance of family, a high regard for bravery in its most corporeal form, an unerring respect for elders, the sanctity of religious teachings and a deep knowledge of, and connection to, the land on which they rely for their very existence. It can be argued that many of the values that the Maasai inherently venerate are also what our so-called advanced Western culture have forgotten.

Yet, in their young lives, Wilson and Jackson have innately recognized the value of certain Western ways. In doing so, the two men automatically place themselves at odds with the ancient, entrenched belief system of their forefathers. In their struggle for reconciliation, they are the personification of an unprecedented connection between the two worlds: modern Western civilization and the rapidly vanishing Mara.

Their home is the cradle of civilization, the land where man first walked. But to view the Maasai culture as primitive is wholly inaccurate. Yes, it is built on centuries-old traditions, practices and beliefs that edges closer to extinction with every new highway that rolls out onto the savannah. But as the story of Jackson and Wilson unfolds, we discover an unprecedented depth and complexity to their lives.

What makes their interwoven life stories even more powerful and timely is that, as they grow from boys to men, from men to warriors, Wilson and Jackson are emergent, prominent figures in their community. These aren't marginal characters with wild ideas: the expectation is that they shall be leaders; guardians of age-old mores and traditions. By attempting to embrace elements of Western culture—from environmental awareness to equal rights for women to education and health issues—they place themselves in direct opposition to their elders, peers and, potentially, their own fate as community leaders.

It's an incredible and prophetic story of courage that is worth sharing with the world—a narrative we have not only come to know but also see, at least in part, unfold before our very eyes.

The day we first met them, Wilson and Jackson made an unforgettable impression. We watched as they took brick in hand to help build a Free The Children school for the boys and girls of their community. The community, historically unaccustomed to allowing girls access to education, looked on as these two powerful, revered and influential warriors literally built a school—unequivocally endorsing equal education for all. It was a turning point for the community. And, for us, it was a telling introduction to two remarkable individuals who would become pivotal figures within our organization.

Both Wilson and Jackson have an undeniably powerful presence. Imagine what it's like to shake hands with a boy who has never been allowed to flinch upon encountering pain; a young warrior who has killed a lion with a spear in order to be considered worthy; an earnest student who has settled a massive, violent revolt by words alone; a man who has stared down drought and starvation. Now multiply that by two.

As warriors, Wilson and Jackson are the last of their kind. And as culture carriers, they are the first. They are certainly the most singularly heroic warriors doing battle today.

This is their story.

Craig and Marc Kielburger
Co-Founders, Free The Children & Me to We

Prologue

When I meet foreigners I am always asked about my culture. "Wilson," they begin, using my Christian name, "What is it like to be a Maasai warrior? What is it like to kill a lion with your spear? To wear cow skins dyed red and manes of lions as headdresses? What is like to be a fierce warrior, among the fiercest the world has ever known?"

I always laugh. "We are indeed warriors. But that is not what the Maasai are really about," I reply. "Let me tell you a story."

Everyone leans in, thinking I am going to talk about windy nights on the savannah chasing elephants and antelope, with our machetes in our hands ready for the kill. Instead, I open with:

"*Taleenoi olngisoilechashur*. There is a saying among Maasai that everything is connected and interconnected. We are all one. We call it *taleenoi olngisoilechashur*."

"Ahh," they say, their expressions showing surprise, maybe even confusion. "Can you tell us more?" someone will ask.

"Well…" I begin, thinking to myself that if they want to hear about lions, I might as well tell them about lions. "Since I was a child, the elders have told me that slaying a lion is as much done with the mind as it is with the spear. When we are in that crucial moment, when our spirits lock, I have one chance, and one chance only, to conquer. If I let my fears grip me for just a second, the lion will kill me. For the lion knows my mind, and I his."

"Oh," they respond, realizing that Maasai culture might be a bit different than they expected. "We were expecting something else. Well, can you tell us about this '*Taleenoi*-word,' then? What is that?"

"Hmm," I say, scratching my chin. "Let me see…I think we should begin this story with Oloruma, our prophet, the *oloiboni*, the one who sees the future."

Chapter 1

Wild predictions:
Wilson and the wise man

For four days all we did was walk, my older brothers, father and I, braving the scorching heats of the Maasai Mara's dry season. This year was drier than ever, with winds kicking up sand that blinded our eyes and temperatures heating up the ground enough to burn the soles of our bare feet. For more than four seasons, our region in southern Kenya had been hit hard with droughts. Our cows, which we depend on for meat, milk and food, were dying from lack of water and grass. As a result, our ribs poked through our chests from famine.

I was about twelve years old. I had taken a semester off from school to help my family move the cows from our *boma*—our homestead, which includes all of our huts and animal enclosures—to the Serengeti in northern Tanzania, where we had heard there was rain and long, green savannah grasses for our herds to eat.

My mama packed up her pots and stirring sticks, and all of our *shukas*, the dresses we wear, and loaded them onto the backs of our donkeys. Then we set off.

Before I was called home, I was away at school. My father sent word to my uncle Rotiken, who I lived with while at school, that I had to leave my classes. "We have too many mouths to feed in our family," he told Rotiken, who then told me. "Some of the other families can survive the drought by selling their cows and sheep and buying vegetables and milk at the markets. But we are too many. We would have to sell everything to survive. So we must move, and I need Wilson to help."

We Maasai never defy our parents' wishes. I had already pushed the boundaries for years with my father, who never wanted me to go to school but had allowed it, begrudgingly. I know he wasn't happy for me to be away from our *boma* spending my days in classrooms with children from other Kenyan tribes, many of whom led more Western lifestyles in their homes.

When I received the message that I was needed to help take the herds to Tanzania, I sadly closed my reading books and gave my math assignments to my uncle Rotiken for safekeeping. "I will come back to school," I told him, "when the rains return."

I smiled when I said these words, but I was choking back tears. For me, school was my passion; and every year since starting school, at about seven years old, I wondered: "Will this be my last?"

"This year, maybe it just might be," I thought as I dragged my feet along the dirt path toward my family's *boma*.

Out in the middle of the Maasai Mara, at the southern edge of Kenya, Tanzania isn't marked by a line or a border with guards checking our passports and giving us permission to enter. For the Maasai, crossing from one country to another comes with just a feeling that we are no longer on the Kenyan side of Maasailand.

But before crossing into Tanzania, my father told me, we were going to stop at the *boma* of the great prophet, Oloruma, one of the wisest men in all of the Maasai Mara. Our elders trusted him to guide them on how to best lead their lives and what the future would bring.

"I want to know," my father explained, his face lined with wrinkles from the heat and the dusty, dry air, "How long this drought will continue and if there is anything we can do to stop it."

"Like kill a particular sheep for Enkai?" I asked.

My father nodded. I smiled.

A part of my mind wanted to believe that the Maasai ritual of slaughtering a sheep for Enkai, our God, as a sacrifice, to get her to bring rain, actually worked. But I had been at school for many years. There, I studied science and geography. I knew that global warming was the real cause of our droughts, and no matter how much we prayed and honoured Enkai, only environmental change would really help bring back our rains.

I put my arm around my father's shoulder. "*Papai*, I am sure the *oloiboni* will know what to do," I whispered in a consoling voice, for my father had never set foot in a schoolhouse and knew nothing about environmental change. "I am sure the *oloiboni* will help us."

When we arrived at the *boma*, my mother and sisters were invited to prepare our evening meal and sleep in one of the *manyattas*—the buildings in the *boma*—belonging to the wives. My father, older brothers and I, however, would sleep outside with the cows.

We made our way to a clearing close to the *manyatta* and created a makeshift *boma* by constructing a thick, round fence out of white bush, orange croton and acacia branches. The cows would spend the night inside the enclosure, the thorns on the bushes separating them from their predators—the lions that roamed the open fields at night.

When we were done, the moon was low in the sky—bright, round and full. The children of the *manyatta*, along with my younger brothers and sisters, began singing.

I followed my father to Oloruma's *manyatta*. It was the first time I was allowed to see the prophet, let alone take part in one of the ceremonies in which he predicted the future.

I was nervous as I entered the dark, smoky hut. Only the dying coals of a fire set deep in a cement hole in the ground lit the main room. One of my brothers had told me that if the *oloiboni* did not like me, or if he felt I was bad or had a bad future, he would single me out.

"If he really doesn't like you," my brother had said, "he will tell you to leave. Having to single you out in a prediction is the worst thing that can happen to a Maasai…even worse than losing a cow."

Although there are many prophets among the Maasai's seventeen different language groups, the one who represents my dialect, *purko*, is the great-great-great-grandson of Agoolonana, who made a crucial prediction generations earlier, one that the Maasai everywhere followed. To this day, many credit Agoolonana with the very survival of the Maasai.

You see, there are forty-two tribes in Kenya. But we, the Maasai tribe, have always stayed pretty much on our own out in the Maasai Mara. We would raid cows from the Kipsigis, our nearest neighbours, but that was pretty much our only contact with non-Maasai. And our Maasai prophets usually predicted whether these raids would be successful or not, for almost always someone would be killed in the conflict.

One time, however, when our ancestors visited Agoolonana, he didn't talk about the upcoming raid. Instead, he drew some squiggly lines on the ground and said a long snake was going to come between the Maasai and the other tribes.

"Can we hit the snake on the head and kill it?" a young warrior had asked.

"No," the prophet replied, "for this snake is not a real snake. It is a big black snake and it is bringing something white with it. It is bringing both good and bad. I don't know what type of snake this is. So be careful. Be very careful."

"What can we do?" asked another Maasai warrior.

The prophet stood up, waved his arms and drew a line right through the snake he had drawn on the ground. "This represents our Maasai lands on one side, and the rest of the lands on the other," he said. "This line is a border," he continued. "The snake cannot pass this border. If it does, the Maasai will be invisible to it."

What came to pass is that the snake represented a highway, and that highway brought with it the British colonialists, who connected the tribes of Kenya through education, commerce and politics. We Maasai didn't assimilate, however. The line Agoolonana drew in the sand came to represent a real line that now runs for hundreds of kilometres through the forests and over the mountains of the Great Rift Valley. The line is so long it is said that Enkai, in the heavens above, can see it. And that line is where Kenya ends and the Maasai Mara begins.

I felt privileged to finally be in the presence of the *oloiboni*, but also very frightened—I didn't want to leave home for good because he didn't like me!

In the *manyatta*, I sat on the bed made out of lantana camera and white bush leaves, squished in beside my two older brothers, both initiated warriors, while the *oloiboni* began the ceremony. He first blessed the local brew my mother and my father's other wives had made, and poured it into plastic teacups, which he passed to the elders in the room, including my father.

After taking a long drink, Oloruma broke into song.

"We were so successful on the hunt, we came home with two lions."

"*Aaraposhoki osinkolio loo ngishu*," the others in the room sang, when the *oloiboni* paused.

"I marched into the *boma* with the lion's mane and tail, to be greeted by my generation, so pleased, so pleased," the *oloiboni* continued.

"*Aaraposhoki osinkolio loo ngishu*," the others repeated. Everyone, except me, seemed to know what to sing. They'd all been here before.

When the big yellow plastic container of brew was finished, Oloruma was given another. Not once, however, did we stop singing. Sometimes the *oloiboni* would sing the chorus. Other times, he initiated the songs.

When his eyes were finally red from drink, and his movements slow, as if he was in a trance, he took white chalk from a small leather bag he wore around his neck and drew wide circles around his eyes. He then drew lines on his hair and on the foreheads of the senior elders in the room.

"And for the prettiest girl," he sang while doing this, "I leapt for her and made her smile."

"*Kitederrie oloiboni nelo entara Meeishaki enaibon enkop niki-yieu,*" everyone sang.

Then abruptly, the singing stopped. The *oloiboni* had put his hand in the air. The room fell eerily silent. The only sounds were the crackling of embers in the fire and the crickets rubbing their legs together in the long savannah grasses.

Oloruma started singing again, but this time, it was not a song. It was a prophecy:

"The drought will end after one complete cycle of all the full moons. The cows will return to their lands and you will have food."

"And you," he then said, pointing his walking stick at me.

My back straightened. I stopped breathing as his dark brown eyes peered into mine.

"And you," he said again, as I reached to touch his walking stick, like the others had done when he had pointed the stick at them. My hand shook as I did so.

"And you," he repeated, as my fingers felt the smooth wood. When he had pointed the stick at the other Maasai, he had done so merely as a way to bless them. He hadn't said anything to them.

"And you," he said a fourth time, as I held my shaking knees. "You will one day work with the white people. You will bring our story to non-Maasai people. You will be our bridge. The bridge of your generation to the world."

I exhaled, letting go of all my fears that the *oloiboni* would say I was a bad person, and then inhaled all my excitement and held my breath. We Maasai are taught as young children to never show emotion, so I needed to hide how I felt.

As the *oloiboni* returned to singing, my mind turned to my life, as someone who was now part Maasai and part Western schoolboy. I thought of my teachers and my lessons, both on the Mara and in the classroom, and how the two differed yet also merged. Then I thought of Jackson, my closest friend. There was no way I was going to do what the *oloiboni* predicted without him.

Chapter 2

Blood brothers:
Jackson meets a new friend

My name is Jackson, or at least that is the Christian name I took on when I started school. I am Maasai. I grew up in a *boma* located on a flat part of a hill in Kenya's Maasai Mara. From the front door of my mother's *manyatta*, I could see the snow-capped mountains of Tanzania.

Wilson is also Maasai but the *boma* where he was born was very far from my own, as long as two full days' walk.

My *boma* was located near a forest. When I was a child, our area received a great deal of rain, which made our grasses tall. Our cows could grow strong and healthy. Wilson, on the other hand, came from a dry, barren area of the Maasai Mara, full of sand dunes and no shade from the sun, whose rays would burn the top of children's heads by the time they reached the hot spring to help their mamas with laundry.

I first met Wilson when we bumped into each other on one of the many dirt paths that wove their way through the rolling hills of the Mara, alongside forests full of yellow bark acacia trees, *olo nini* shrubs, bush babies, monkeys and, of course, lions. We were both about seven years old and lived with our uncles while we went to school (my uncle was Jonathon and Wilson's uncle was Rotiken). Jonathon and Rotiken's *boma*s were close to each other, about a forty-five-minute walk from Naikarra Primary School and about an hour's walk from the town of Naikarra.

I knew Rotiken long before I met Wilson. Rotiken was a Maasai elder, a wise and revered man. One time, when he visited my family's *boma*, he shared with us that for sixteen generations the Maasai elders believed Wilson and my generation would be special. It was nighttime, and Rotiken's almost-black eyes stared into the flame of an oil lamp set on the table in front of him.

"How so?" I had asked.

"Hmm," he replied, pausing and looking up to the ceiling to find the right words. Then Rotiken shifted his large frame and his eyes, which softened when he looked into my own.

"The wise men of long ago predicted that the times in which your generation would live would be different," he began slowly. "There would be wars and famine all over the world—and for the first time, the Maasai would know about the happenings in these very faraway lands. There would be droughts not just in the Maasai Mara, but in all of Africa, ones that would threaten the lives of all our cows. Many young men and women would move away from Maasailand in search of knowledge and ways to earn money to survive. These Maasai would integrate with and marry non-Maasai. The elders of long ago believed that our entire culture could be in danger of extinction.

"But the Maasai warriors of your generation were born for these times," Rotiken continued. "It was prophesied that you and your brothers would encounter non-Maasai people while also ensuring that our ceremonies, traditions and values are preserved. It was prophesied that you would tell the stories of the Maasai and of our traditions to the world. And that, in fact, the result would be the opposite: our culture would become more solid, as the world began to embrace some of our traditional ways of thinking."

On the very first day Wilson and I met, I had forgotten Rotiken's story and I was just a typical, eager kid. We were both walking the path to school. We eyed each other suspiciously. He grunted a hello, while I fingered my *conga*, the stick we Maasai carry as a weapon that looks like a small cane with a giraffe's head on the top.

"Who are you?" he asked, raising his hand and pointing a finger at me. "Where are you from and where are you going?"

Wilson and I were barefoot, carrying our black school loafers tied together by the shoelaces around our necks, and wearing the same school uniform: a pair of blue pants and a red cotton button-down shirt.

"My name is Jackson and I am going to school," I blurted out. "Where else do you think I'd be going dressed like this?"

"What are you going after?" he then asked, pointing at my *conga* and the stones, which I had been throwing into the fields, and now gripped in the palm of my other hand. "A lion?"

My eyes shifted side to side. "Yessss…a lion," I replied, trying to appear brave. "Some warriors chased two lions into the forest over there a few days ago," I continued. "They killed one, but the other got away." I then asked, "What is your name?"

"Wilson," he said, as his big, dark brown eyes grew even larger. He took a few steps toward me. "Shall we go look for the other lion?" he asked, pulling his *conga* from his black leather belt.

I nearly flinched but I stopped myself in time so Wilson wouldn't see my fear. Maasai boys never show they are scared or in pain, for such reactions are seen as shameful to them and their families—even to their entire villages!

But truth be told, I had never seen a lion, and I was a little afraid to meet one for the first time with another boy, not an initiated warrior with experience killing the creatures. I wasn't about to tell Wilson that, however.

"Okay," I replied, bravely. "You know what to do?" Not waiting for a response, I started reciting what I had learned from my older brothers about what a Maasai warrior should do when he meets a lion. "You never want to look right into the eyes of a lion," I told Wilson, hoping he'd think I'd done this before. "If you do, then the lion will know it is you who wants to pierce its skin with your spear. If a lion senses you are going to attack, it will attack you first. What you want to do is look past the lion, keeping it in your side view," I said, mimicking the action. "Dance around a bit, leap from foot to foot, and then *bang*—throw your spear with all your might."

"I know, I know," Wilson spat, walking right up to me and punching me in the shoulder. "Stop dawdling! Come on. Let's go!"

Wilson and I raced along the path, then out over the long savannah grasses. Every now and then, I would catch Wilson, whose legs were much longer than mine, looking at me. I knew what he was thinking: "How can this little guy run so quickly?" You see, I was half the size of any Maasai boy my own age, but quicker on my feet and more adept with a football than anyone.

As we neared the forest, we were neck and neck and speeding up, not slowing down. Sweat started to form on my forehead. I had been warned my entire life to never go into the forest without initiated warriors by my side. It didn't appear that Wilson had been given the same information. Or, if he had, he didn't care. But then, at the edge of the forest, he stopped suddenly.

"Okay, you win," he said.

I sighed and stopped too. As we caught our breath, we stood side by side, looking into the thick foliage.

"I think the lion is probably gone," Wilson eventually said. "Maybe we should turn around."

"Yes," I replied with a serious tone, trying not to reveal my relief. "The lion will be long gone by now, probably back with its babies. And we don't want a pink slip from the teacher for being late for school."

Our conversations after that, at least for a little while, were mostly made up of huffs and grunts and single sentences at a time. What I didn't let on was that I was nervous of Wilson, and a little jealous. He was confident and brave. He was not only strong, but had a good eye. He could whip a stone from in-between his fingers with such force and precision that he could knock a bare-faced, go-away bird from a yellow bark acacia tree more than a hundred strides away. He could also pierce the skin of a candelabra tree, causing its thick and acidic sap to spurt out in all directions. I didn't want him to think I was an inferior Maasai, so I said very little. And I tried to keep up to him in everything we did together.

It would be many years before we were in the same class together at school, but we would frequently meet on the path on the way home to our uncles' places. Occasionally, we made *congas* together out of wood from *Olea Africana* trees. We then used those *congas* on other boys who dared to cross us.

"You are the Kipsigis," Wilson would shout at the boys. "And we," he would say, puffing up his chest and pointing to himself and then me, "are Maasai. You have our cows!"

"And we are going to come and get them!" I would add.

Wilson and I then chased those boys, throwing our *congas* and whipping stones at their heels trying to make them trip. When one did fall, we would tap him on the back and say: "One cow. I got one cow back from you. You are dead. Now remain on the ground until we catch the others."

Ever since I could understand my native language, Maa, I had heard the elders telling stories around the fire at night about how the Maasai are the rightful owners of all the world's cows. Enkai created the Maasai and cows at the same time. Now, the Kipsigis, the tribe that has always lived the closest to the Maasai, they had cows, too. But they didn't need the cows to live on. They grew vegetables and fruit trees on places they called farms. They mostly used the cows to till the land. This action was unacceptable to the Maasai and a useless waste of a cow's potential.

The Kipsigis cows *belonged* to the Maasai, and I grew up hearing the stories of how my ancestors would raid nearby Kipsigis villages and take their cows. These raids started off with giving a prediction on how the raid would unfold, and often ended in battles between the Kipsigis and Maasai men, in which some would inevitably be killed.

Wilson and I re-enacted these raids with other children, and we usually won. We would chase any boy who came onto our path, with our eyes enflamed, our bodies pulsing with energy, chanting our mantra: "We are taking our cows back!"

Of course, when we got to school, we would hide our weapons and wipe the blood away from any injuries we sustained so as not to show the teachers we had been fighting. And we'd all pat each other on the back in friendship.

Four years after our first meeting, Wilson and I were friends, but not close. The rivalry that started with the running race between us to see who would stop first before entering the forest had continued. We even competed over who got top marks in school. It was usually him, but I was a strong second...and I did better than him in math.

The first time Wilson and I found ourselves in the same class at school was in Grade 5. I was about eleven years old—but, unlike the non-Maasai students in the room, I was not exactly sure how old I was. I'm still not today. Neither is Wilson. The Maasai don't record the day and year a child is born. We don't use the Western calendar, which I came to depend on at school to tell me when I had a Swahili vocabulary test or a math quiz. The Maasai tell time by the cycles of the moon, and our ages by the generations we are born into, also called our age group sets.

Wilson and I were of the same generation, which encompasses boys born within a span of about fifteen years. Anyone born in the same generation, the start of which is determined by the elders, is considered the same age. Every Maasai boy takes part in several initiations and ceremonies, until they graduate and become a man. One of the most important rituals is living in a cave with other young Maasai boys of the same generation and slaying a lion. Wilson and I hadn't lived in the cave yet.

In our Grade 5 class, Wilson and I shared a long wooden desk that was so old the wood was deeply chipped, making the table impossible to write on without piercing the paper with our pencils. Wilson usually sat on the aisle side, so he could see the teacher, Mr. Kimathi, whose desk was in the middle of the room, while I strained to lift my neck up over the other students' heads to see the front chalkboard.

Our desk was located at the back of the classroom, closest to the door, which remained open except on the windiest and rainiest days of the wet season. When the door was open, I often found myself staring outside, watching the wind kick up the sand, daydreaming about being on the football pitch, running in bare feet down the field and kicking the winning goal for the regional championships.

One day, I was in the midst of such a reverie when Wilson's laughter pierced into my thoughts. I turned quickly to see him jumping up and down in his seat. (Wilson was the class clown. And one of his favourite antics was to fling his hand into the air whenever the teacher asked a question.) "I know! I know! I know," he was saying in between his bounces and giggles.

"Okay, Wilson, who was the first president of Kenya?" asked Mr. Kimathi, a stout man who wore bright red bow ties with his short-sleeved, button-down white shirts.

The problem with Wilson was that half the time he had no idea what the right answer was. I always knew when he didn't. When the teacher called on him, a few trickles of sweat would form on his forehead and the fingers on his right hand would start tapping the bench beside him, exactly like he was doing now. But what amazed me about Wilson was that he always belted something out nonetheless.

"Daniel Moi, sir," Wilson answered.

Wilson continued to smile a wide toothy grin, as Mr. Kimathi's face turned to a scowl. "Wilson," he spat, "I've asked you a dozen times: if you don't know the answer, don't pretend you do. Give others in the class a chance."

Our schoolmates, almost all from the Kipsigis and Kikuyu tribes, began to laugh. Wilson, loving the attention, stood up, bowed and said, "Thank you. Thank you. Thank you," as our classmates clapped.

"Detention, Wilson. After school," Mr. Kimathi boomed, as everyone went quiet. "You'll clean the chalkboard brushes, and you and I...we'll have a little talk after that."

The attention of the class moved to Mari, a tall, slim girl with plaits in her hair who sat in the front row. "Kenyatta," she said shyly, twirling her pencil around in her fingers as Mr. Kimathi nodded. "Mzee Jomo Kenyatta. He was the first president of Kenya."

Mr. Kimathi ended class by announcing that for Monday, he wanted everyone to read the chapter in our history book on Kenya's independence from its colonizer, Great Britain, and to complete an algebra assignment from our math book.

I heard thunder off in the distance and turned quickly to look out the window. Its glass was cracked in the corner from a misdirected football. Lightning filled the western sky, and a shiver ran through me. I felt as if something bad was about to happen. I usually didn't wait for Wilson to walk home. But this time, I sensed I should.

"Meet me in the library when you are done your detention," I whispered to Wilson, as the other students packed up their things and got ready to leave. "It's going to be wet on the path when the rain comes. Let's go together."

"Yes," Wilson whispered back, as if he too sensed something ominous.

In the library, I read my homework assignment to get it out of the way so I could spend the weekend walking Jonathon's cows. At one point, my mind drifted from reading the words on the pages to listening to the rain, which sounded like wildebeest hoofbeats on the school's tin roof. Another shiver ran through me as my thoughts turned to the Mara River, which we would soon have to cross. "We have done it in the rain many times before," I reassured myself, thinking of the large boulders that spanned the breadth of the river, allowing Wilson and me to leap across easily. "Even in the rainy season, when the rocks are slippery, we manage just fine," I said out loud. I shook off my fears and returned to my reading.

Wilson eventually arrived, snapping his fingers and smiling.

"How was it?" I asked, as he tossed his wet book bag on the floor and dried off his arms and legs with a towel.

"Same as usual," Wilson replied, beaming. "Mr. Kimathi told me not to distract the class anymore. He told me about the importance of reading and writing and respecting others. Then we ended my detention by talking about traditional Maasai medicines. One of his children has malaria and he wondered if I could bring some leaves from the East African greenheart for his wife to boil with water and give to the child, to help her heal."

"You are lucky!" I exclaimed. "Anyone else who gets in as much trouble as you gets suspended from school, maybe even permanently. You walk out with a pat on your back because you get such high grades and help those who are sick!"

"I am lucky, I guess," Wilson said with a wink.

Wilson and I then spent about an hour completing our homework assignments. When the rain eventually began to subside, we prepared for our walk home. We took off our good leather shoes and rolled up our slacks so they wouldn't get muddy. Then we wrapped our canvas book bags and shoes in plastic.

When we stepped outside, we were hit immediately by the wind. It was so strong and wild we couldn't hear each other speak. We walked side-by-side in silence, our heads lowered as we pushed ourselves against the gales.

At the football field, we stopped to collect our *congas* and machetes, which we had hidden behind a tree. We then headed down the dirt and stone road toward the path that led to our uncles' *bomas*.

The path was muddy, like I had feared, but when we reached the first hill, our toes dug in and gripped the mud.

I began to feel confident that all would be fine. Until we came to the Mara River, that is.

It was raging. The water was much higher than usual because of the rain. Dark clouds made the dusk sky appear like night, without a moon and stars to light the way. Although I could make out that the river was full of rough, white-capped waves, which made it difficult to even gauge the locations of the rocks we needed to jump on.

Wilson went first, and he leapt onto the first rock with success.

But just as Wilson's foot was about to land on the second rock, a big wave crashed into him. As he fell into the dark water, he managed to grab the rock with his fingers. He held on tight and slowly pulled himself up.

Safely crouching on top of the rock, he looked around, shook his head and turned back.

"We're not going to be able to do it," he shouted into my ear, when he was on the riverbank again. "Let's go back to the school."

But the school, like the sky, had become black. All the staff had left for the weekend. The janitors, who were also nowhere to be found, had padlocked the doors to the classrooms. We walked around the compound of one-storey cement buildings until we found one classroom open. Inside, I took off my shirt as Wilson slipped off his drenched pants. He then wrapped my shirt around his waist like a skirt.

"If we s-s-stay here for the weekend," Wilson said, his teeth chattering from the chill of being in the river and the cool air, "we will have no food or fresh drinking water until Sunday night, when the staff return."

"We have to get across the river somehow," I replied.

We decided to cross at a different location, one where the river was not as wide and the water was a little shallower, and started out for there.

It was now pitch black outside. But Wilson and I grew up in the Maasai Mara. Our *bomas* never had (and still don't have) electricity, so we are used to getting around at night. We can usually hear and sense when our predators, like lions and green mamba snakes, are near. But on this night, we heard nothing but the howling wind.

When we reached the part of the river we wanted to cross, my heart sank. It, too, was full of white-capped waves, and the rocks we hoped to leap on to get from our side to the other were partly submerged.

Wilson and I looked at each other and, without speaking, knew what to do. We cut down a young and thin yellow bark acacia tree. Working fast, we stripped off all the branches with our machetes. And still without a word spoken between us, we headed back to the river. All the while, my mind was churning. Wilson and I didn't know how to swim. If we made one wrong move, we would drown! We would both be swept away in the raging current, our bodies submerged and thrown up against the rocks until we died.

We heaved our book bags through the air all the way to the bank on the other side of the river. Wilson then slowly slipped his body down into the water, until he was touching the bottom. Only his head and shoulders remained above the surface. As I followed him into the water, he held on tight to the root of a tree at the riverbank's edge. Once we were both in the water, we stretched the pruned acacia tree from the first rock to the next, making sure it was held tightly in place by the force of the rushing rapids.

Very slowly, we walked our way along the bottom of the river, gripping the tree with one hand and holding tight to each other with the other in case one of us lost our footing. At each rock, we stopped and moved the small tree farther along. We worked our way across the river without words, as if our minds had become one.

When we finally reached the last rock, Wilson took the small acacia tree and jammed it into the side of the riverbank so it would be steady. We then grabbed hold and took our final steps to safety.

Up on the far bank, sitting beside our book bags and catching our breath, we looked into each other's eyes.

"From this day onward, let's support each other to be the best we can," Wilson shouted over the wind.

"We are brothers now," I replied.

"We are!" Wilson shouted back. "Me! You! Together!" We clasped each other's hands. "United!"

Chapter 3

Brave beginnings:
Wilson emerges

I was born in my mother Kerempe's *manyatta*, which was made out of mud and wood. My mom grew up with my father, Rureto, my father's four other wives and my forty-two brothers and sisters. I was born in Engosuani, near Mararita, where my father and mother spent their childhoods. Mararita was annexed into a game reserve when they wed, so they moved to Enkare Nairoua. Since they couldn't return directly to Mararita, as the Maasai are not allowed to live on game reserves, they chose a nearby village when I came into this world.

Before I could walk, we moved back to Enkare Nairoua, which had once been a lush region of the Mara, but was now very dry. Amidst the sand dunes, however, remained the most beautiful oasis in all of Maasailand where I bathed in the hot springs, collected stones and skipped them along the smooth surface of the water, and helped my mother clean clothes and bathe my younger siblings.

I wasn't named when I was born, for we Maasai are never named at birth. Maasai children take part in a naming ceremony when they are tall and strong enough to watch sheep on their own and accompany junior warriors as they take the cows out to pasture. (That would be about five years old, in Western terms.)

The Maasai believe our names are sacred. Children die young out in the Mara, where life is rugged. We have no electricity and no heat sources other than our fires. There are predators including lions and diseases like malaria, typhoid and cholera. If I was to die before reaching my warriorhood and I had been given a name, that name would have to die with me. No one else could ever use it.

But if I was an old man and I died? Well, then it would be an honour for a child to inherit my name, for I would be a senior elder, which is what we call those with wrinkled, sagging skin and crooked knees and backs, whose minds preserve our stories and *olngetiai* or myths.

Like all girls and boys, my milk tooth was pulled when it grew in, as is Maasai tradition. Of course, I didn't flinch or grimace. It had been drilled into my head by my older male siblings since I could crawl that Maasai boys can never show pain. Girls could cry when their tooth was pulled, but I could not.

I was brave in everything I did back then, so brave that by the time I was about four, I led other children out into the bush in search of the strongest, thickest *leleshwa* sticks to burn each other with, a tradition among young Maasai boys. When we returned with one, we would place the stick—which had white and green bark—into the fire. We'd let it heat up and then hold the end of the stick on an arm or leg for several minutes. When it was removed it would leave an open wound, which would eventually scar. I had so many of these scars I lost count, and I hadn't even been named yet.

As boys, we did this to toughen us up for our circumcision ceremonies, which take place when we are much older. Burning ourselves is seen as a way to master our strength, in not flinching or showing pain. My older brothers said I was going to be a strong and fierce warrior, perhaps the strongest and fiercest of all, because I was so brave.

My fondest times, as a young child, were when my uncle Rotiken would visit and tell me stories. We would sit by the fire, with the sounds of hyenas laughing in the distance, or sometimes the roar of a lion, and Rotiken would tell me about Maasai life. Initially, his stories were always about the animals of the Mara, and my future role with them.

"When you are old enough to go with the cows," he said once, his long staff drawing lines on the ground just as the great prophet Ago-olonana did long ago when he predicted the snake, "lions come out in the morning or at night, but never in the middle of the day, for it is too hot for them. They sleep during the day. Now, lions," he continued, his voice deep and hoarse, just like I imagined a lion would speak if he could talk, "often sleep in the forest. Don't ever, ever go into the forest alone. Don't take the sheep there, don't take the cows there and don't go looking for medicine like *Olea Africana* to mix with soup to make it tastier, unless you are with a group of initiated warriors. Chances are, you could wake one of those lions. And if you are alone, they will kill you, easily, for they have fear of you, too. If you lose a cow or if a cow wanders into the forest, turn back and have a group go in search of it. Never go by yourself."

"The lions are afraid of me?" I asked, wide-eyed. It was not possible that such a great beast would be frightened of me, a small child.

Uncle Rotiken nodded and then continued. "Well, maybe not the female lions. You see, male lions are lazy. If they come near you or the cows, they're usually just acting as decoys. Their goal is to turn the cows' and the Maasai's attention toward them, while the females slink around in behind. Always it is the females of the pride who do the kills. Even if she is afraid of you, she will never be too afraid to attack."

"What about the leopards?" I asked.

"Ahh, the leopards," Uncle Rotiken replied. "They are harmless to the cows. But they can kill a sheep or a goat. If you see a leopard, take off your blanket and chase it away. Make lots of noise, scream, yell, sing, jump up and down, and swing your bright red blanket over your head and run right toward it. It will leave."

Rotiken also told me about Agoolonana and his prophecy about the snake.

"But why was the snake not good?" I asked Uncle Rotiken, when he finished the story.

"The snake was the highway," he explained. He took his spear and drew in the dirt the same design the prophet had drawn.

"Like the one out there," I said, pointing beyond the dirt path my brothers used to take the cows out to pasture and, during drought, to Tanzania, in search of green grasses. "That's a road?"

"Yes," Rotiken replied, his eyes narrowing. "And that road has an animal on it that runs on gasoline and can carry as many as ten people at a time inside its stomach. The road is called a highway and the animals take those non-Maasai people from Nairobi, a big city, to Tanzania. Most of these animals, which are the size of elephants and are called cars, trucks and *matatus*, carry good people. But sometimes these animals carry people who are very dangerous to us."

I leaned forward and held my breath as Uncle Rotiken paused.

"The police," he finally said, in a stern, strong voice. "The police drive in cars and trucks and vans on that road, and if you ever see them, run!" I didn't know what this word "police" meant. But Uncle Rotiken's tone of voice indicated that they were something to avoid.

My mother told me the same thing when I told her about my conversation with Uncle Rotiken. "How will I know the animal is carrying these people called police?" I asked.

"Doesn't matter," she replied. "If you see a car or truck coming, you are to run until you have no breath left in you," she said, kneeling down so our eyes were at the same level. She then grabbed my shoulders and shook me gently. "Hide in the hot spring, if you can make it that far. Hide under the sand. Just run and hide wherever you can."

Shortly after that, Uncle Rotiken visited but he didn't whisk me into his arms, like he normally did. Instead, his face was sombre and he shook his head at me and said, "Not now. I need to speak to the elders."

Rotiken and the elders walked out into the field and, forming a small circle, spoke in such soft voices the wind couldn't carry their words. Their faces were grave, and a few times they pounded the ends of their spears on the ground in anger.

"What is going on? What is going on?" I asked Uncle Rotiken when he returned.

"The police got the sons of Ole Karia and Ole Lepore," he told my *papai*, who was standing behind me. "Rounded them up like we do the cows for branding and took them away to school. We may never see them again."

Of course being a Maasai, I couldn't show fear. I just nodded, as did my father. We said how sorry we were and then I returned to watching the sheep. But when I was alone that night, behind my mother's *manyatta*, I allowed myself to sit down and think about what Rotiken had said. With my arms folded over my knees, I bent my head and sobbed quietly.

I had enemies, I thought to myself. And they weren't just lions. They were police who took Maasai children away from their families—to this place called school.

"Jambo, habari ya leo?" a friend said, a few days later.

I tilted my head and scrunched up my face. "What did you say?" I asked in *Maa*.

"I said, 'Hello, and how are you today?' in Swahili, one of the official languages of Kenya," he proclaimed.

My friend, who was about two heads taller than me and also didn't have a name yet, was from Turere, a *boma* about a half day's walk from my own. I hadn't seen him for many, many moons. He had grown tall and somehow had managed to exchange his baby fat for lean muscles. He also spoke words I did not understand.

"How did you learn that?" I asked, as the two of us heated up burning sticks to use on each other, as this was what my Maasai friends and I often did when we started playing.

"At school," he replied matter-of-factly, which startled me so much that I nearly dropped the burning stick into the fire. "I go!" he said with a smile. "And you should too."

"What is this thing called school that I hear everyone speak so badly of?" I asked, placing the heated end of my stick on my friend's thigh.

"School is where I go and learn Swahili, the history of Kenya and how to count. Look," he said, pointing to the ground. "How many rocks are at our feet?"

I stared at where my friend was pointing. "I don't know," I replied. "They're just rocks!"

"There are five rocks there. How do you know how many sheep you have? How do you know if one goes missing? Do you count them?"

"Count—what is this thing? I know my sheep by their colours, by the shape of their faces, by the way they 'baa.' I know when one is missing because I can't see it anymore."

"But when you become a Maasai warrior, you will have to take so many cows out to pasture...your cows, your father's cows, your uncle's cows, your mother's cows. You can't memorize what they all look like. Counting can help. And I learn counting in school," my friend boasted, patting me on the back.

From what Uncle Rotiken had said, being taken away to school was something to be feared. So I was really confused by what my friend was saying.

After he and I finished burning each other, neither one of us flinching of course, we headed to the fields. While we watched the sheep, he taught me some words in Swahili, including *wewe ni mwanafunzi sasa* (you are a student now). After that, he taught me how to count my sheep, 1...2...3...10...12. I admitted to myself, but not to him, that I did find it was easier to keep track of the animals when I counted them, rather than memorizing their colours and shapes.

That night, after drinking some cow's blood and milk, I asked my mother if I could go to school.

"No," she spat, putting down the beaded wedding necklace she was making for one of my sisters. "This is no place for you to go. If the police take you to school, we will never see you again. If you see the silver or gold animals, the size of an elephant, coming toward the *boma*, you must run," she admonished. "And run far. Far!"

"But my friend sees his mother and father and he goes to school," I retorted, standing up to my mother for what was probably the first time in my life.

My mother's nostrils started to flare and I could see her face becoming flushed. But then she shook her head slowly, and sat down with a sigh. "I know," she said. "But he is different. He is somehow an exception.

"You see, long, long, long ago, many generations ago, people who were not Maasai came to the Mara. They had dark skin, like ours, but looked different and spoke in languages we had never heard. They learned our language and said they wanted to take our children away. A few times, our ancestors trusted these people and gave them our young. They never saw the children again. And then our ancestors heard from the Kikuyu, who had lost lots of their children, that all of Africa was experiencing this. Our children, our mothers, our healthy fathers and young men, were disappearing on ships located off the western shores, ships sailed by people with white skin. Our ancestors vowed that the Maasai, from then on, would have nothing to do with these foreigners, black skinned and white."

Rotiken had spoken to me often about this time in our Maasai past. He said that it was called the slave trade and Africans were taken from their villages, across a great water, to the West Indies. He said the slave trade brought a blanket of more than just sadness, but grief and horror, over the entire continent of Africa.

And so when Agoolonana drew that line in the sand, which exists to this day in the Great Rift Valley, the Maasai listened. They remained in isolation from the rest of Kenya and the world. They stood alone.

I knew all this. But at a young age I was also aware, from overhearing elders in conversation, that times had changed yet again. While I had never met them myself, I had heard that tourists, with white skin, were coming to the Mara to see our animals, and found the Maasai fascinating because of our bright clothing and beads, and because we lived in *bomas* and drank milk and cow's blood.

I had also overheard Rotiken and some of the elders chastising Maasai leaders for giving parts of the Maasai Mara away to the foreign companies bringing in the tourists. I even heard some of the elders say that maybe we should start sending young Maasai to school, so they could learn Western ways and become better leaders, to better protect our land and our culture.

"Please, I want to go to school," I cried out to my mother. "I know about all the African children sent on ships to the West, many dying on-board the vessels, others dying from abuse and overwork. But my friend goes to a school near his house. He sees his mother and father. He likes it. He says it is good. Please let me try?"

"No," my mother said, stomping her foot and then repeating: "When you see that silver or gold animal, as big as an elephant, coming toward our *boma*, you run. You run very fast and very far!"

For many moons after that I would wake in the night, gasping for air, thinking of these people, the police, and imagining what they would look like. A giant, maybe, like Olarinkoi, whom Rotiken would tell me about one day.

Then my fear turned to want, as I thought more about what school could be like. I felt deep inside that somehow, this place where my friend studied was where I was meant to be. I tried to push the thought away, but it always returned, particularly in the middle of the night.

Finally, a few moons later, my attention turned to something else. My mother announced that I was old enough to be named.

The next day started with a hush that fell over our house. I woke in the morning, headed to the river to wash and then spent the day with another mama, not my own. For the first time in my life, my mother didn't let me tag along as she milked the cows and fetched water from the river. Another mama did my mama's chores, while she and my father spent the rest of the day in her *manyatta*, speaking so quietly I couldn't hear a peep when I tried to eavesdrop below the opening in the wall that allowed the smoke from the fire to escape. No one was allowed to enter, including me.

"They are discussing your naming ceremony," my father's third wife told me. "And your name."

"I bet you get a good strong name," whispered my brother, who was about the same age as me, "because you are big and strong and never flinch."

"And because your mama loves you very much," another brother added.

I felt warm inside hearing these words. My mother had many children. My father, who had three wives, had many more. My mother would always say to us *Kaanyor ikeraa anei pooki* (I love all my children) and pull us into her long, strong arms and hold us tight.

That night, I drifted to sleep hearing in my dreams my mother, who I called my *nini*, singing me the Maasai lullaby, as she often did when I was a baby.

My mother and father's discussions about my name and naming ceremony lasted from sun up to sun down and for several moons. Finally, they emerged from the *manyatta*. But instead of life returning to usual, they headed immediately to the *boma* of Ole Kiok, a tall and slim senior elder with a short white beard.

I sat outside his *manyatta* playing with a stick on the dusty ground, and tried to listen to their conversation. But I couldn't hear a peep.

"We know what you are trying to do," my mother called out at one point. At that, I stood up with a huff and headed back to my own *boma*.

The moon waned until it almost disappeared from the sky, and the women in my *boma*, including my mother, my father's first wife and my older brothers' wives, began making the local brew. "It takes several suns to prepare," my mother told me, as we went off into the fields to find the aloe vera that would be fermented to make the alcohol. Then she added, "When the brew is ready, you will be named."

The women stirred the local brew in big metal pots over small fires. The air slowly filled with the scents of aloe vera and honey. The women who weren't making the brew cleaned the *manyattas* and looked after the young children.

I watched in awe. Everything was alive. Everyone played a role in this first of several initiations I would go through before I would become a warrior. And mostly, their tasks were performed without a word being spoken between them. It was as if the women were of one mind, and just knew what roles to play.

Chapter 4

Leaning on ceremony: Jackson's early days

My birth, so my parents say, was auspicious. The midwife stood outside my mother's *manyatta* and announced over and over again, "We have a baby. We have a baby!" Saying this five times meant that my mother, Arami, a well-known and beloved Maasai herbalist, had had a boy. If the midwife had said "we have a baby" fewer than five times, it would have meant Arami had had a girl.

When I was born on that starry night in the middle of the dry season, my mother says I didn't cry, which was a good sign. "Maasai warriors never cry or show pain," she would often tell me, as young as when I first cooed in her arms, and then as I grew into a small boy and would sit by her feet. "And you, my little future warrior, you didn't cry at all!"

My father says that I came into the world to the sounds of the wind howling over the swaying grasses of the Maasai Mara, kicking up dust and sand into swirling cones that blinded the warriors out watching the cows. But it was okay, he said, because these swirling cones usually meant rain was on the way—another good sign.

After I was born, my father slaughtered a sheep for some fat, which I sucked on to help me grow big and strong. My mother was also given some of the fat and the juiciest parts of the meat so she could make the best milk of all. In Maa, cow meat and fat mixed together is called *olpunda*, and this is all Arami ate for weeks, in addition to drinking some milk and cow's blood.

My mother's *manyatta* was located to the left of the main entrance to my father's *manyatta*, indicating she was the second wife, for the first wife always lived in the mud and wood hut located to the right of the entrance.

After Arami gave birth to me, the midwife boiled some grated bark from the euphobia tree with water and used it to clean the afterbirth from both my mother and me. I spent my first night nestled in my mother's arms in a bed made out of *leleshwa* bush branches and leaves from the *lantana camara* bush, which smelled like eucalyptus.

Like Wilson, I was not named when I was born. And the year and date of my birth were not recorded, for Maasai don't follow a calendar. We know when a year has gone by through the passing of the seasons, rainy and dry. We distinguish one month from another by the waxing and waning of the moon. On the night I was born, it was a half moon, and my father's favourite cow, a black one with a white spot on its back—another auspicious colouring for a Maasai cow—gave birth to a calf. "This is an omen," my father told my mother, "that the son in your arms will be great."

I grew big and strong drinking first my mother's milk and then cow's blood and milk, mixed together in a calabash. Then, when I could crawl, I was given elimanet, which is clotted cow's blood, to suck on.

This was my diet, morning, noon and night, until my legs were strong enough that I could roam the savannah with other children from my *boma* (the children of my father's other wife) and the surrounding *boma*s and pick the fruit from the trees, including the *olmorijoi*, also known as the poison arrow, and the *teclea*.

But for the Maasai, the cow, its blood, milk and meat, has always been the food we depend on. One of the very first stories I recall a senior elder ever telling me was about Enkai, our god. Enkai is the god of rain, sun, love and fertility.

The cow could talk, and once Enkai had left, the cow told the Maasai man: "Enkai made me to be your food."

"But if I eat you, you will die," replied the Maasai.

The cow told the man to tie its neck and then pierce the vein with the tip of a spear. "Collect some of my blood in a cup and then tie the wound, so it stops bleeding. I won't die. After that, drink the blood," the cow explained.

"When you need meat," the cow continued, "boil the blood and when it cools, it will harden and taste something like meat."

"What about fat?" the Maasai asked the cow. "How do I get fat?"

"Take my milk," the cow said. "Let it turn into cream, and then you can drink that. See? You don't need to kill me to get the food you need."

"What about bone marrow?" the man asked. In Maasai culture, babies are given bone marrow to help them walk and grow strong and healthy.

The cow pondered the predicament. "This will be very difficult," the cow finally said. "The only way for you to get my bone marrow is for you to kill me. I guess that must be the way, because Enkai told me that I was your food.

"I will not speak anymore. I will moo instead. Then you can kill me for my bone marrow and not feel guilty. Without a voice I am beneath you. We are no longer equals."

The Maasai was saddened, but he too knew there was no other way. The cow stopped talking and the warrior eventually killed the cow to get the bone marrow his children needed to grow tall and healthy.

I always dreamed of the day I would be able to eat real slabs of meat, dripping in juices, just like the warriors, for small Maasai children don't eat meat. I grew so impatient watching the warriors chew on the bones after a wedding or naming ceremony that one day my brother and I—the son of my father's third wife, who also didn't have a name yet—decided we would take some for our own.

I was about four, in Western years, and the occasion was the circumcision ceremony for a boy from another *boma*. My brother and I snuck after the men, and watched as they slaughtered a cow by tying its four legs together and then stabbing it with a knife on a soft part of its head. The men let the blood drain into calabashes, and then cut away the flesh to take some of the bones and then bone marrow. After that, several men carried the carcass to a clearing in the bush where they began cutting it into parts and roasting it over fires.

Children could watch the men kill the cow, but were not allowed to see the cooking of the meat, so my brother and I hid. We peered out from behind a massive olive tree and saw many senior elders sitting on the ground, drinking a local brew the women had made. They drank this brew only on special occasions. The younger men did the roasting, stretching the pieces of leg and ribs across sticks, and then sticking them in the ground, close enough that the meat would cook.

I was wearing a green *shuka*, and it flashed, catching the attention of my older brother, Koimeren, who came running over to our hiding spot. He pulled my younger brother and me out from behind the olive tree by the backs of our *shuka*s.

"What are you doing here?" he shouted in Maa.

I started to say we were collecting *rhus natalensis*, a herb for my mother's medicines, but no words came out. My mouth was dry. All I could think about was how my father had warned me that children would be caned if they ever went into the bush to watch the men prepare their meat. Or worse, they would get a visit from the pinching man, called in to discipline Maasai children who don't obey their parents, by pinching them hard, all over their bodies.

"We wanted to see what you were doing," my younger brother blurted out, stunning me with his honesty. I thought for sure that Koimeren was going to hit us both on the back of the head with his *conga*. Instead he laughed, a big hearty laugh that drew the attention of the other men, including some of the elders—who surprisingly didn't seem to mind that we were there.

"Yes," I said, not wanting my younger brother to get all the credit for being brave enough to tell the truth. "I, too, wanted to see how you prepared the cow for the feast so I could learn for when I am older."

"Well then," said Koimeren, still holding me by my *shuka*, "come and try some."

Koimeren let go of my *shuka* and had us follow him to a small fire, on top of which sat a big metal pot. My older brother dug a metal fork into that pot, full of steam and boiling water, and pulled out what looked to me like a long slithering worm. "The intestines," Koimeren stated with a wide grin. "The tastiest part of the cow. Try it," he said, passing me the fork.

I started to move my hand up to take a piece, but hesitated.

"Ahh, coward," my older brother hissed, shaking his head. "You are no Maasai warrior if you have fear."

"I am not afraid," my little brother pleaded, grabbing the long piece of the cow innards. "Ow," he said, letting it go. "It's hot. It burned my hand."

Koimeren's eyes grew wide. "Two Maasai cowards!"

Koimeren again grabbed us by our *shuka*s and dragged us off to an isolated part of the bush. "You are lucky it is just me cooking the intestines, and that only I saw you afraid to eat it. You will bring shame to our family if you ever show fear again," he said directly to me. Koimeren then hit us both on the head with his *conga* and sent us back to eat the intestines.

The piece I took was long, and Koimeren laughed as part of the intestine hung down from my mouth, past my chin and onto my chest. I paid no notice. I chewed and chewed and chewed, and soon it was all gone. Koimeren was right. It was good. Delicious, even! My little brother and I then scurried back to our mamas, our heads hurting and our pride wounded, but our bellies full of our first taste of cow.

Life as a Maasai boy was about being tested. Constantly. My training to be a warrior began when I could walk. My father would take his cane and hit me across the back of my legs. If I didn't cry, I was on my way to being a good warrior. If I did, I would be caned again and again, until I stopped crying.

Then, when my two lower centre teeth, which we call the *ilala len-kule*, came in, they were immediately removed. Both boys and girls have these teeth pulled once their baby teeth are fully in, and then again they are pulled, when the permanent teeth are formed. The Maasai do so as a way to differentiate themselves from other tribes. It is cosmetic, for us, and a sign of beauty.

When my milk teeth were pulled, I had to sit on the ground and allow my mother to pull them out, starting with her loosening each tooth from the gum using a small machete. All the boys from my *boma* and surrounding *boma*s crowded around and watched, their eyes pinned to different parts of my body to make sure I didn't flinch or show any form of pain or discomfort. After both teeth were out, I was given some milk to wash out the blood and nothing else, not even medicine made from the *rhus natalensis* tree, which was a pain-killer. I had to endure the pain. And since I did, and didn't cry, I was given my very first goat, a red one, and a white sheep.

"My son will be a good warrior because he didn't flinch," my mother said to the other mamas, beaming as I scurried off down the savannah to watch my father's sheep with the other children. "A very good warrior!"

Many of my evenings as a child were spent by the fire, near the *boma* where the cows spent the night. A great senior elder—called an *elpayiani-kituak*, or wise man—often visited. A wise man sees and understands the past to guide Maasai in the present, I came to understand, while our prophet foretells the future. It was through this *elpayianikituak* that I learned much about the Maasai. It was the *elpayianikituak*, for instance, who told me about how we build our *manyattas* to encircle the cows' *boma*, which is located in the middle. "The goal is to protect the cows from lions," he said. "The entire purpose of being a Maasai warrior is to protect the cows. You are nothing to your community if you can't do this."

"How did we come to be here, in Kenya?" I asked once, just before my naming ceremony. The old wise man told me lots about Kenya's forty-two tribes, including the Kipsigis who lived on the other side of Olengoloto Mountain.

"And we steal their cows!" I piped up, for ever since I could talk I had been playing raid-the-cow games with the other children.

"It is not stealing," the *elpayianikituak* said, shaking his head and resting his chin on his smooth black staff. It was made from an olive tree, which indicated he was a senior Maasai elder. "Cows belong to the Maasai. When we go on our raids, we are merely taking back our cows."

He then returned to telling me about the Maasai as a tribe, and how we live among the rest. "I cannot speak for the other tribes, but we Maasai are nomadic, which means we travel around a lot," the *elpayianikituak* continued. "We have always moved, and still move with, our cows to find them greener and greener pastures. Our *manyattas*, even today, are built with mud and sticks, so we can just leave them behind whenever we move. They are easy for the women to rebuild from scratch, when we find new places to live.

"I've heard some say that we Maasai are one of the ten lost tribes of Israel," he continued. "We made our way down to Sudan, and then travelled into Kenya in search of these green lands, past Mount Kenya, to our final resting place here, in the Maasai Mara and the Serengeti of northern Tanzania. The Maasai Mara and the Serengeti are collectively known as Maasailand."

At that point I changed the subject completely, my mind racing ahead of me. There was so much I wanted to learn from him, so much I didn't yet know. "And what about the sheep, *papai olegeni*?" I asked, using the term young children use to address wise men. "Enkai created the cow. But what about the sheep I watch during the days? Who created them?"

"Enkai created everything," he replied. "And Enkai created the sheep after a heavy rain. At the end of the rain, a Maasai warrior walked out of his *boma* in search of food. When he reached the river, he saw, sitting in the middle, a big black animal. The Maasai waded in and picked up the animal, which he called 'sheep.' Not far down the river, the Maasai found another sheep in the middle of the river, but white. He took them both back to his village and told everyone, 'Look what Enkai brought us. A black sheep and a white sheep!'

"'And what are you going to do with those?' asked another Maasai.

"'Care for them,' the Maasai replied.

"Not long after that, Maasai started to sacrifice sheep whenever there was a drought," the great elder explained. "When we needed rain, we killed one sheep and offered it up to Enkai, to thank her for bringing us the animal to begin with. The very first time the Maasai sacrificed a sheep, rain came within five minutes."

"We found our beads in the river, too," my mother said, walking up behind me and touching the back of my neck. She must have been listening to our conversation. "Many generations ago, the mamas used shells they found in the riverbeds and fish eggs for beads. We Maasai women," she said, running her long delicate fingers over her bracelets, "like being beautiful. We sew the fish eggs and shells together with cow or sheep gut to make our necklaces, earrings and belts. And one day, you will wear a special bracelet to indicate the generation of warrior to which you belong."

"I can't wait!" I exclaimed.

My mother smiled. "Good," she whispered. "The first thing we need to do then is prepare for your naming ceremony."

"You mean it is time?" I asked, wide-eyed.

"Yes," my mother said with a laugh. "Your *papai* and I will start making the arrangements when the sun next rises."

Chapter 5

All in a name:
Wilson and his Maasai identity

My childhood, on the Mara, was idyllic. I spent my days playing a *boma* game with my friends. We made miniature *manyattas* out of mud and rocks, created the cows' enclosure in the middle with sticks and used pieces of yellow bark acacia tree for the fences that lined the entire complex. We then scoured the ground underneath the savannah grasses for crystals, which we would use to represent our sheep and cows. If I would find a shimmering white crystal or a dark black rock, I jumped for joy, for these corresponded with the best colours of cows. An all-black cow with one or two white spots, or an all-white cow with a few black spots, is seen as spiritual and blessed.

"This one is my bull!" I would yell across the savannah, at which my brothers and friends would come running, tackle me to the ground and try to take the crystal from me.

Naturally, the goal was to have as many cows as we could, and we would spend half a day, or longer, crawling along the ground and underneath shrubs and bushes to find the perfect rocks and crystals to represent my herd. Sometimes my herd was so big the cows' enclosure alone was twice the size of my friends' *bomas*. This is when I was seen as the richest Maasai among my friends.

At that point, my little brother would become jealous and strike up a fight: "Shall we have a battle?" he would say, pulling out from his belt a little *conga* my dad had made for him.

"You want my cows?" I would say, my chest puffed up, my eyes flashing. We would stare into each other's eyes until one of the girls intervened.

"No fighting!" she would say, jumping between the two of us. "We only fight the Kipsigis for our cows, not each other. Has your mama not told you that yet? We Maasai never hurt or harm each other."

The girls played *boma* too, but their role was to look after the babies, represented by tiny rocks, and to clean the *manyattas* with water they would collect in calabashes from the river.

Our *boma* game usually ended with one of the mamas from the nearest *manyatta* calling out for her child to come. "My young baby," she would say, for none of us had a name. We would glance furtively from one person's face to the other, and then point to each other.

"You...You! I think she is calling you," we would say in unison.

Then we would all run toward the mama, who, with her hands on her hips, would glare at us as we approached. Standing right in front of her, she would swat our heads with a branch from the orange leaf tree. "None of you are going to get a name," she would scold, "until you can look after those sheep properly." We would all turn and look at the sheep, which we had left alone near our abandoned *boma* game. "I will tell all your mamas," she would then say, pointing to the boys in the group. "That you don't know many things and are not good warriors."

The mamas were always saying things like this to us when we were young. The purpose was to make us wise.

When the day of my naming ceremony finally came, I found myself to be sad. I was awakened at sunrise, when the rooster called for the third time, by my father shaking my shoulder. I rubbed my eyes, full of sleep, while he wrapped a green blanket over my *shuka*. He then took me out into the field and let me choose a sheep, which he said would be slaughtered for the ceremony. My pick was a big fat white sheep, which my father said was a good choice. "A pure sheep, the colour of peace, the colour of the pure Enkai," he said as he led the sheep to one of my brothers, who took it into the forest to be killed.

When I returned to the *manyatta*, my mother sat me outside on the ground and shaved my head. She nicked my skin a few times, but I did not wince. "From now on," my mother explained as she shaved, "you will wear your hair short. Only the unnamed wear their hair long."

As my curls fell to the ground, I bit my lip and swallowed back tears. I felt that in some way my childhood days of playing *boma* were over. While I was excited for my warrior life, which lay ahead, I was also afraid, though I dared not voice my fears. I was afraid I would not make a good warrior. I was afraid I would not be strong enough and I would let my family down. I wanted to run back into the field and play with the rocks and make-believe creatures, instead of the real-life ones that would soon be my responsibility.

My brother Kasaine came up to say hello, shaking me from my melancholy, just as I was nicked by the razor blade. Of course, I showed no pain, nor did I flinch. Kasaine exclaimed, "He'll be good in the cave and with the lion one day." I wanted to smile, but held myself back. I was taught to never show fear, but I had also been told to never show pride, which is also considered shameful.

When I was completely bald, my mother took some red dye, made from red soil mixed with cow or sheep fat, and rubbed it into my head. "Maasai are superior to all other tribes in Africa, for we are fierce and strong," she explained. "When we wear red on our bodies, we are feared by everyone. And we use the red for ceremonies because it is believed that the red protects the wearers from foreigners." When my *nini*, Maa for mother, had finished, she dyed the head and face of my father's first wife, followed by her own. They were both dressed in their best beads, including their marriage necklaces.

My *papai* explained to me that a woman always presided over Maasai naming, circumcision and marriage ceremonies. "It is believed that the Maasai woman who gives the blessing represents Enkai," he said. "It is also believed that Enkai's attributes of kindness and love, strength and softness will be passed on via the woman to whoever is on the receiving end of her blessing.

"Today that is you," he said, nodding at me. He too had his head dyed red.

I popped inside my *manyatta* and saw my older sisters preparing *chai* and *chapatti* for everyone to eat. And it was a lot, because people were coming from *bomas* far and wide to celebrate my naming. They were gathering outside my *manyatta* and on the fields.

Some of the oldest men dipped their calabashes into the local brew the moment they arrived, so that by midday they were stumbling when they walked, propping themselves up with sticks and then tumbling over. "That brew does strange things to people," I whispered to my mother, who laughed.

"When you were a baby, you were given the bone marrow of an elephant," my father said, changing the subject. "It is very difficult to kill an elephant, so being given some of its bone marrow means you are special. Very special."

This time, I didn't care that it was shameful to show pride. I smiled.

My father led, followed by me and then my mother, as we made our way in a line to the centre of the cows' *boma*, where the woman chosen to preside over the ceremony stood. We stopped in front of her, and I found myself quickly surrounded by male and female elders. Ole Kaputa, a wise man, stood beside the woman and held a calabash with *olo nini* plants attached to the side.

The wise woman, who is called an *ikatengenak* in Maa, asked my parents: "What do you think of the name Miton Ole Meikuaya?"

I lowered my eyes and wracked my brain. "Miton Ole Meikuaya. Meikuaya was my grandfather's name, that much I knew. He died when I was just a baby, but I remembered being told that he was a great man, with a great heart. He was part of the delegation of Maasai elders in Engosuani who would visit the *boma*s in the community and make sure those who were in need were cared for. When necessary, he would call for a *harambee*. The *harambee* is a Maasai tradition in which everyone contributes to a local pot to help those in need, so that those who had lost cows due to drought or lions, for instance, could buy more.

The Maasai don't believe that the spirits of those who have died come back. But somehow I always felt that my grandfather was with me; sometimes I even heard his voice, telling me to be a good child, a good person.

The woman asked my parents three times what they thought of the name Miton Ole Meikuaya, and all three times *nini* and *papai* said nothing. Then, on the fourth time, my parents both nodded and my mother whispered, "*Ee*," which is Maa for yes.

The whole group then said: "Bless his name. May the name be with him always!"

Ole Kaputa drank some of the local brew from the calabash and spat it out in the fire beside where we stood. "I want you to be with your name forever," he said to me. "Miton Ole Meikuaya."

That night, the stars seemed to sing and the crickets rubbed their legs together a little harder than usual, creating an orchestra of music, as if they were joining the warriors in their songs of slaying lions. At one point, my mother slipped around my neck my very first necklace, a single strand of tiny yellow, red and white beads.

When the sheep came out, cooked by the men in the forest, I was given the breast and asked to eat first. The meat was soft, rare and bloody. I feasted on *chai*, *chapatti* and the sheep so much my stomach bulged. And my eyelids eventually began to close from fatigue.

But as I was making my way to my *manyatta* to sleep, my father pulled me aside and asked me to follow him. When we arrived in the cows' *boma*, well lit from the various fires from the ceremony encircling their enclosure, my father pointed to a big black cow with a white spot on its back. "Black represents Africa," my *papai* told me, his hand resting on my shoulder. "And white represents peace. I give to you, my son Miton Ole Meikuaya, this beautiful cow, which represents both Africans and peace. You are on your way to becoming a Maasai warrior." He beamed as my eyes and energy perked up and I moved to touch my very first cow.

"Your journey, Miton Ole Meikuaya, has just begun."

Chapter 6

Halt, police!: Jackson and his strange encounters

My mother, Arami, started the preparations for my naming ceremony. I was excited because Arami was an *ikatengenak*, a wise woman, and would be presiding over my ceremony. As one of the most respected medicine women and midwives in the Naikarra region, she would be the person to give me the blessing of my name.

For days leading up to my naming ceremony, I could not sleep. I would wake in the middle of the night, the coals of the fire nearly chilled, and slip outside. Dew would be settling on the grasses and the stars would be twinkling, singing the soft lullaby that keeps the babies asleep through the night.

I would sit on the damp ground and run through all the possible names I might be given. Many Maasai children born in the night, like I was, are called *Leteipa* or *Lekaarie*, for in the evening or in the night. Those born during the day are often named *Ledama*. Some Maasai children are named after animals, like *Oltome*, which is Maa for elephant.

In the end, I gave up guessing. I threw my hands up into the air, saying, "Enkai, I leave it with you and the stars to decide my name. I will accept whatever is given."

When my parents eventually left to visit the senior elder, I knew my naming ceremony was close. But instead of getting excited, I began to feel afraid. That same day my parents left, another elder arrived at my *boma* and told my father's first wife that the police were close, very close, within a day's walk, driving animals the size of elephants. They were taking all the children, she said—all the children around my height.

My mother had warned me that the police might come. "We have seen parts of our land, which belongs to all Maasai, sold by greedy and corrupt Maasai businessmen and leaders, who pocket much of the money for themselves," my mother had explained to me, shaking her head, her eyes steely cold. "Stealing, other than us taking back our cows, or dishonesty of any kind, is not the Maasai way. Promise me one thing," she said. "If anyone ever tries to steal you from us, including those police, run...run... run like the cheetah."

The chill that had settled in my bones that day deepened when I learned that the police were now so close. And just a few moons later, after my parents were back, that animal, which really was the size of a male elephant but green, like a *dobeya* forest, finally made its way toward our *boma*.

I ran like my mother had told me to, imagining my stout legs to be supple and strong, like the antelope's. I ran and ran, until I felt a cramp in my side and could run no more. I skidded in behind a giant yellow bark acacia tree. Following quickly on my heels were four other children from my *boma*.

The others curled their bodies up into little balls, and caught their breath, while I poked my head around the big tree and watched as men descended from the sides of the elephant-like animal, including someone who wore a red *shuka* and plaid blanket.

"A Maasai," I gasped. "The policeman is a Maasai!"

Some of the men went into the *boma*. I could not see them once they passed by our fence made out of *leleshwa* bush. But two others, including the Maasai man, strayed out into the field. The Maasai man stopped, and his eyes scanned the savannah as if he knew where we were hiding.

I stretched my head and neck as far as I dared, and kept my eyes glued to him. Suddenly, the Maasai turned, looked right at me and pointed his finger.

My heart beat so fast, I thought it would leap out of my chest. I pulled my neck and body back behind the tree. "Run," I mouthed the word to the others, but nothing came out. I'd lost my voice. Fear had gripped me.

My mind churned. "What do I do? What do I do?" I thought. I am a Maasai. We do not become afraid. "But I am afraid," I thought.

Finally, I hit myself on the head with my little *conga* "You are a Maasai, do what you do best," I admonished myself.

"Run!" I finally yelled at the top of my lungs to the four other children. "Run!"

We scattered in every direction: two ran toward the *boma* at the bottom of the hill, another ran up the hill and the fourth child and I ran toward the forest we had been told never to enter.

"Either the lion will get me or the policeman," I thought as my legs flew over eucalyptus plants and *olosida* bushes.

But my tiny legs were not long enough. The Maasai man from the elephant-like animal easily caught up to me and, while in full stride, grabbed me by the waist and swung me onto his back.

He carried me all the way back to my *manyatta*, where he plopped me down in front of my mother, father and two of the other policemen.

I ran my eyes up and down their bodies, for they were wearing strange cloth on their legs and arms. And slung over their shoulders were curious-looking weapons, like spears, but with blunt ends. But for some reason, I no longer felt afraid.

"What is that?" I asked in Maa, pointing at the weapon held by one policeman.

"It is a gun," the Maasai policeman replied. "But don't worry, we won't use it on you. It is for the animals, in case we run into any that give us trouble."

"What does it do?" I asked, in a confident voice that surprised even me. Usually, I was very shy when I first met someone, and I had been taught to fear these men.

"It releases what is called a bullet, a tiny metal object the size of a small pebble, with such force that it can pierce the skin of even the fiercest of lions and kill it, instantly."

"Ohh...we should get one of those for the *boma*!" I exclaimed to my mother.

"Do you know these people?" the Maasai policeman asked, waving a hand at my mother and father, whose eyes were lowered, their faces gaunt. They were exuding an energy of pure anger.

"That's my *papai* and *nini*," I said proudly, smiling. But my mother and father were not smiling. My father looked up and flicked his fingers at me, which meant I was in for a beating with the cane after the police left.

"Do you want to go to school?" the Maasai man asked, ignoring my father's actions.

"Maaaybeee…" I replied cautiously, my eyes on my father, who was still flicking his fingers at me.

"I have something that might convince you." The Maasai man dug his hand into a little bag he was wearing around his neck and passed me what felt like a soft rock. It was yellow in colour. The policeman told me to put it into my mouth. "And suck," he said, "like you do the *osilalei* gum from the trees."

I did what he said and within a few seconds I tasted the sweetest juices, sweeter even than the sugar we would put in our *chai*.

My eyes lit up.

"You like!" the Maasai police man exclaimed, laughing. He then got down on one knee, so that his eyes were level to mine. "If you go to school with me, I can guarantee that your lessons will be even sweeter than this butterscotch candy I have just given you. You will like school very, very much."

"Can my mother and father have this thing…a caandii?" I asked. But when I looked at my mother and father, they shook their heads and scowled. "Nooo," I began, turning back toward the Maasai policeman. "They don't want a candy, after all."

"Mr. Policeman," I continued, with trepidation, "my father is going to cane me when you leave. He may even call for the pinching man. Please take me with you. I want to go to school. If you promise that I can come home again. I don't want to leave my parents forever. But I'd like to try this thing called school that some of the other children have told me about."

"I have every intention of taking you with me," the Maasai policeman said, putting his hand on my shoulder. I felt some relief at his words, for I knew I had avoided a beating at home. Yet I also felt a shiver of fear run through me. What if the others were right and I would never see my *boma* again?

"I do promise that you will return home again, very soon," the policeman added, as if he had read my mind. "You see that over there?" He pointed to the elephant-like animal. "That is a jeep. Go hop in the back and I will join you shortly."

As I crept toward this animal called a jeep, I overheard the Maasai policeman asking my parents if there were more children. But then the conversation faded, as all I could focus on was the big thing in front of me.

I pulled out my *conga* and swung it in the air in front of the creature to show it who was boss.

My *boma* wasn't located near a road. I had never seen such a thing before.

I slowly tiptoed toward the back of the creature, treating it as if it were a lion by making sure not to look directly into its big bulging eyes. But when I reached the back, I jumped in fright. The creature had another set of eyes!

When I regained my composure, I shuffled my feet forward, tilted my head and looked at the animal's eyes, which were big and shiny, and did not blink. I put my hand out in front of me, closed my own eyes and touched the animal's silky smooth surface. It didn't move. So I slowly opened my eyes and peered into the forehead, which was an open space. I gulped for I could see its entire insides. And in the middle of the jeep were some seats, overtop of which were some plaid red Maasai blankets. "It's eaten some Maasai warriors!" I yelled out loud. "I must go to tell the policeman."

"It's not an animal," said the Maasai policeman, laughing as he walked up behind me. Three of the children with whom I had been hiding behind the yellow bark acacia tree were with him. "It's a machine," he said, as the other children stared wide-eyed at the creature the same way I had. "It can't move until I put these in." He held up some shiny metal objects that clanked together like tiny cowbells. He then moved around to the side and opened a door, and told me to get in. "It won't bite," the Maasai policeman said with a smile. "But it *will* take you to school."

As we left, I looked back at my *manyatta* and smiled. Driving over the savannah, I imagined returning to my *boma* a hero, my father having forgotten all about my defying him by talking to the police. Instead, I would be recognized as the bravest Maasai of all. "He went to school," I imagined the other children saying in awe. None of my brothers or the other initiated warriors I knew had done that. I would be seen as fearless.

I didn't get much time to enjoy the wind rushing through my hair from the open jeep windows. Before I knew it, we were there. "School!" the Maasai policeman exclaimed, pointing to a square building surrounded by a low fence as we drove up to it. My eyes quickly scanned the area. The school was located in a flat clearing in between two forests. Several children surrounded the car when the jeep stopped. I didn't move. My hands perspired and I gripped the red Maasai blanket I was sitting on.

"I thought school was far away," I choked out. My mouth was dry and the words were barely audible.

The Maasai policeman heard, nonetheless, and smiled. "No. The school has always been here, in Naikarra region, what non-Maasai would say is about two kilometres from your *manyatta*. Did no one in your family ever go to school?"

"I think," I said, closing my eyes, "my uncle Kadipo might have. I think he said something, sometime, about going to school when he was a boy. But uncle Kadipo didn't tell me anything about it."

"Does he have a non-Maasai name?" the policeman asked. "Something else people call him?"

"Yes, Jonathon. He told me he has a job, somewhere he goes every day, and while he is there people call him Jonathon. Is that a non-Maasai name?" I asked, wanting to please the Maasai policeman.

"I believe so," he replied, taking my hand as I hopped out of the jeep. "And I think that when he went to school, someone gave him that name."

Suddenly, our small group was swarmed by the small children of the school, two of them took my hands while others grabbed pieces of my *shuka* and took the hands of the three other Maasai children with me. They guided us into what one of the Maasai students said was a "playground" where they played games.

This playground was full of wooden beams and fence-like toys that some of the children were now climbing on and over. Six children remained around me, touching my hair, which was long because I hadn't yet been named, and my green *shuka* and blanket. One of the children, a short boy with round eyes and long, long eyelashes, ran his fingers over the scars from the burning stick that covered my arms and legs. The child turned and said something to the policeman in a language I could not understand.

The policeman put his arm around the child. "He thinks someone hurt you," the policeman said to me. I looked into the boy's eyes, which were cloudy with tears. "I will tell him," he said with a smile, "that the scars on your body are what you did to yourself, and that they are a source of pride."

As he did so, I looked at the children, who were wearing similar pieces of cloth on their legs and arms as the non-Maasai policemen.

"*Jambo sana, jambo sana,*" two young girls cried out as they emerged from the square building and ran toward me. I didn't understand these words. Furthermore, these children spoke very directly to me and one another, not like the Maasai, who speak to each other as if they are reciting a poem. I tilted my head and began looking into the children's mouths when they opened them to talk.

Their smiles were big and wide, their teeth white, but none of them had a missing bottom tooth.

"These children are not Maasai," I thought to myself. "I'm meeting Kipsigis children for the first time in my life. My father will think me so brave to be among the Maasai's enemy."

"The children at this school are not all Maasai," I told the Maasai policeman when he had returned his attention to me. "I was told you rounded us all up from *boma*s far and wide. Where are all the Maasai children?"

"School is made up of children from all of the tribes of Kenya," he explained as he led me into the school. "There are Maasai, but many others too."

My eyes were wide, taking in everything—including the building's construction. It was not made out of mud and rocks, but smooth stones, piled one on top of another. It also had a flat and smooth stone floor, not dirt, like Maasai *manyattas* had. And the school didn't have a hole in the wall for the smoke from the fires to breathe out of. Instead, there were many holes. I walked over to one, and banged my head.

"Ow," I said, rubbing my forehead where it hurt.

A tall, slim man, wearing cloth on his legs like the students did, entered the school and smiled when he saw me. "It's glass," he said in Maa. "You just hit your forehead on glass."

"I...I...I don't understand," I stuttered.

"You will understand everything soon enough," he replied warmly. He then introduced himself as Mr. Olelekarpoi, the only Maa-speaking teacher at the school. "A teacher," he explained, anticipating my next question, "is a person who helps you learn how to count and read."

He told me to follow him to the back of the room, through a door like I had only ever seen before at the market, to yet another room. Sitting at a long wooden table were ten children, all about the same size as me, whose smiles revealed missing bottom teeth. My eyes lit up. "These are Maasai!" I said enthusiastically, as they made room for me to sit beside them.

That night I ate my first non-Maasai meal: *githeri*, which is made up of tiny pieces of vegetables floating in a liquid. "These are carrots," said one of the Maasai boys, pointing to the orange items.

"And tomatoes," said another, pointing to the red pieces.

"And they grow in a garden, which we will show you after we eat."

"So we don't have cow's blood and milk at school?" I asked the Maasai policeman, who was standing nearby, watching us.

"No. Only Maasai drink cow's blood. You will soon learn that there are many different foods and meals in Kenya. And they are all good," he said, rubbing his stomach.

That night I slept on the floor of what would be my school during the day.

When the rooster crowed for the third time in the morning, we Maasai children, being the only students who stayed in the school, rose and pushed the tables and benches out from the walls and back into five single lines. Then we headed to the cleaning house in the back, where I washed my hands and cleaned my teeth with a stick with a tiny brush on the end and strange-tasting paste that stung my mouth.

The Maasai teacher, who told me to call him Mr. Olelekarpoi, gave me a pair of what he called pants, which were blue. They were exactly like the odd-looking cloth the children and the policemen wore on their legs. He showed me how to put them on, then handed me a red-coloured shirt. I couldn't do what he said were "buttons," so he helped. He then gave me a pair of black shiny shoes, which were made out of cow hide and had strings up the front. He slipped them on my feet. "Comfortable?" he asked.

I shook my head. I had always gone barefoot. "My feet feel cramped, like the cows must feel when they are in their branding corrals."

He laughed. "You can take them off when you are outside and at night," he said. "You just need to wear them when we are in class. And you will get used to them!"

Mr. Olelekarpoi took my *shuka*, my blanket, my small machete and my *conga*. "When you go back to your *boma*, you can have these," he said. "But at school, we wear what you are wearing now. It is called a uniform."

At first, I didn't understand a single thing my teacher and the other students said in school. I was sitting beside a non-Maasai child in the third row. Every so often, he would shoot his hand up in the air and reply to something the teacher had said. The Maasai boy sitting on my other side explained that the language he was speaking was called Swahili. "I didn't understand it either, when I first arrived," he then added. "But I do a little now. You will get it soon enough."

To me, Swahili sounded like a song—"sola, sola, sola, sola,"—whereas Maa, which involved clicking our tongues against our upper mouths, sounded more like "tick, tock, tick, tock."

Everything was so new to me, but soon I began to fall into the school's daily routine. We usually had *githeri* at midday and for evening meal. For breakfast, we had a heavy substance called *ugali*, which I rolled in the palms of my hand until it was sticky. Slowly, ever so slowly, like the Maasai boy who had been sitting beside me, I began to learn Swahili, and became confident enough to say a few words in the language at mealtime.

"*Jina lako ni-nani?*" I asked a girl, whose long hair was plaited with multicoloured ribbons tied at the ends. "What is your name?"

She blushed, so I continued. "*Habari yako?*" ("How are you?")

"Fine," she said with a smile. "I feel fine."

And it wasn't only Swahili that I was learning. Mr. Olelekarpoi taught me about time. "When the moon followed by the sun is complete, this is a day," he explained one day. "A full moon cycle, of one full and one invisible moon, is a month. Thirteen cycles of the moon is a year. And all of the non-Maasai children at school count the years since they were born and celebrate the day they came into the world, usually with a big sweet cake, made of sugar. This is their age, and every year they celebrate what is called a birthday, on which the child is a year older and given presents."

"A cake!" My mouthed watered, for the school's cook had given us a cake just the night before. This cake had chocolate icing, which melted inside my mouth and tasted even better than the butterscotch sweet the Maasai policeman had given me.

"Every day has a name," Mr. Olelekarpoi continued. "And we repeat that name every seven cycles of the moon."

"Oh," I said with a sigh when he was done. I didn't really understand these words, "month," "time," "day." In fact, I wouldn't really understand everything that Mr. Olelekarpoi would tell me that day until much later.

Every afternoon as the sun began to set over the mountains of Tanzania, the non-Maasai children would head to their *bomas*, which they called homes. We Maasai children left behind would head to a big field where we played a game called "football." Mr. Olelekarpoi, who remained at the school at night with us, taught us how to play.

He would always cheer me on. "You have a gift," he told me after a game one day. "The way you move down the field, so fast, so strong, and you've only just learned how to play...you are better than anyone else out there. Maybe one day you can play for the Kenyan national team!"

I didn't know what that was, so I just smiled.

"So," he continued. "I understand you didn't have your naming ceremony before you came to school."

I shrugged. "*Nini* and *papai* were starting the preparations for it."

We were sitting on the grass, and watching the other Maasai students head into the school for the evening meal.

"You know, in school, all of the Maasai children have Christian names, like Spencer and Susan, and Jonathon...like your uncle."

"How did you know about Jonathon?" I asked.

"Because we have been speaking with him," he said. "He lives about a forty-five-minute walk from here, through the hills over there." He pointed to a path.

I blinked. Mr. Olelekarpoi had also been teaching me and the other Maasai children about Kenyan time. So I knew what forty-five minutes meant.

"Tomorrow is Friday," he continued "And there is a break now for many cycles of the moon. You are going to live with Jonathon. He has agreed for you to stay at his *boma*, and to show you how to get to school when it starts again, and how to get home every day and on Fridays for two days straight, which we call the weekend."

I sighed. "It is true. I won't see my mother again?"

"No," Mr. Olelekarpoi said, rubbing my back. "Jonathon will take you to see your parents when you live with him. But Jonathon and I feel that if you return to your father's *boma*, your mother will not let you return to school. I went to visit Jonathon myself, who explained to me that he had completed Grade 8 and he wanted you to do the same. He promised he would make sure you attended and help you raise any needed school fees, such as for your uniform."

I held back some tears. "Mr. Olelekarpoi," I eventually said, "I thought I was finished with this school. That I had completed what I needed to do. Do you mean I have to come back?"

"Yes," he laughed. "For many, many years! You are just going home now for a break, to see your family, and then you will return.

"But you need a name," he added matter-of-factly. "A Christian name. I would like to give you one. Do you have any ideas?"

My eyes grew big. "I get to choose my name?"

"Yes, you can choose your Christian name, which we will use at school."

I could think of nothing.

"I have a name for you," Mr. Olelekarpoi said after a long silence. "What about Jackson? The best football player this school has ever seen was a boy named Jackson, who went on to university and became a teacher. And you are the best football player I have ever seen since him. So what about taking on his name?"

"Jaaakson." I ran my mouth over the word. "I like it," I called out. "I like it!"

Jonathon came to the school the next day and said that while I would be living with him and going to school every day, at this point I wouldn't be returning for about a month. "It's a holiday," he said. "And I am going to take you to see your mother and father. Your *nini* is very worried about you."

"How long have I been away already?" I asked.

"About a month...one full cycle of the moon."

"How come I am going to live with you?"

"You can live at your *boma* on holidays like this," he said. "But because the police don't trust that your mother and father will send you back after the holidays, I will come and get you and you will stay with me when school is on. The police and the school officials think your *papai* and *nini* will just hide you away. All of the other children caught in the raid of your *boma* are gone. They've disappeared. Their mothers and fathers came and got them from the school, and now they are living somewhere else. The police don't know where. But I want you to go to school," he said, wrapping a new red, plain blanket around my bare shoulders. "And I think I have convinced your parents that school is important."

"Why?" I asked, my feet now bare, enjoying the feel of the earth between my toes.

"Because I went to school, I was able to get a job doing storekeeping. I have money that I can use to buy food and water, which is needed when we have droughts," he explained. "You will see I live in a cement house, like the school, which does not have a leaking roof during the rainy season, and it has a door in the front that opens and shuts, keeping the chickens out. My new wife and I have no children and we want you to be our son."

I gulped. I knew it was a great honour to be chosen as someone else's son. But I also knew I had to ask my mother and father first. "Thank you," I told Jonathon. "You are a very kind man."

Jonathon took me along the path that I would soon walk every morning on my way to school and, every afternoon, home. It was the same path on which I would meet Wilson. And the same path that lined the forest full of lions. I would walk it to and from school for the next eight years.

Jonathon didn't stop at his *manyatta* when we passed it. Instead, he took me directly to my *boma*.

That night, I told my *nini* and *papai* about all the things that happened at school. They just glared. "What is this name you have been given?" my mother said, her eyes narrowing.

"Jackson," I said proudly. "He was the best footballer when he went to the school and the Maasai teacher says one day I will be, too!"

"That is not a Maasai name," my father said with a scowl. "We'll talk some more about this school thing and living with Jonathon later—"

My mother finished the sentence: "But first, you have to have a Maasai name. No son of mine is going to be called a name like Jackson without a Maasai name of great honour coming first."

And so, during that very first summer holiday from school, I had my naming ceremony.

Chapter 7

Getting schooled:
Wilson's early learnings

I, too, ended up at school—the same one-room schoolhouse in Naikarra that Jackson attended. And I got there first. When we look back, Jackson and I estimate that we may have missed each other by only a few moon cycles, for it was in the dry season of the year I was about age six that the police raided my *boma* and rounded up seven children, including me, and took us to school.

Jackson arrived at the end of the rainy season, perhaps of that same year. But by then I was in Grade 1, not preschool.

Grade 1 was part of the elementary school, which was located a few football fields away from the preschool. The elementary school was made up of many small cement-block buildings, set across from each other along dusty walkways. To the south was the football pitch. Tall acacia trees kept the ground cool in the dry season and us dry in the wet season as we raced from building to building.

Because my *boma* was many days' walk away, I slept on the school's cold cement floor for three complete cycles of the moon, one full cycle in the Maa calendar being fifteen days of darkness, and fifteen days of light. That is a Western month, I came to learn, so I spent three months living at the school before my uncle Rotiken came to get me.

Uncle Rotiken lived only forty-five minutes from the school, and not far from Jackson's uncle Jonathon. Rotiken had spoken to my parents, who had agreed to let me live with him while I attended school, in much the same way Jonathon would be watching over Jackson. My *papai* and *nini* were not pleased to have me go. But Rotiken is a wise man and he told them it was time for the Maasai children to begin learning some Western ways so we could become leaders among our people.

One Friday afternoon, with a warm breeze tickling my cheeks, I held my head high and walked out of the school grounds barefoot, wearing my *shuka* and carrying my *conga*, and traversed that dusty path for the first time, over the hills to Rotiken's place.

In Grade 1, I threw myself into learning Swahili, and then English, which I wasn't supposed to be learning for a few years. But during recess time, when the other children would walk along the wooden beams in the playground or head to the football pitch, I would sit cross-legged on the ground underneath the open window of an English class and listen in. Eventually, my Grade 1 teacher, Mr. Kariankei, caught on. "I didn't see you during break. Where did you go?" he asked me outside the classroom one day.

I shrugged him off and waved. "Nowhere," I replied in Swahili, which I was learning quickly.

"Wilson, I saw you," he said, a twinkle in his eye. "I've seen you for the past week. Why do you want to learn English so much?"

"I like the way it sounds," I replied. What I did not tell him was that I just knew I had to study the language. Somehow it would help me later on.

"If you want to learn so badly," my teacher continued, "sit right in on the class. I've already asked the teacher. He said it is fine for you to do so."

I thanked Mr. Kariankei, but instead of heading into the classroom, I paused. As a Maasai boy, I had been brought up to always respect what my elders said and never speak back. But there was something really bothering me that I felt Mr. Kariankei could help me with.

I swallowed hard and mustered up the strength to ask him for a name. "Mr. Kariankei, everyone in the school has an English—or what you call "Christian"—name, except for me. No one can pronounce Mei-kuaya. They call me Moocooaa," I drew out the syllables, puckering up my lips and making a sound like a cow.

Just at that moment, Mr. Mbogua, the English teacher, rounded the corner. He stopped when he saw me.

"Did you tell him he can come to my class?" he asked Mr. Kariankei in Swahili.

"Yes," said Mr. Kariankei. "But Meikuaya was explaining that he doesn't have an English name and he would like one."

I shifted my feet from side to side and lowered my eyes. I felt I was about to be in trouble, perhaps even caned, for speaking out. Instead, Mr. Mbogua placed a warm hand on my shoulder. "Son," he said in Swahili. "My closest friend is a Maasai warrior. His English name is Wilson and he went to school, too, all the way up to Grade 12. Do you like the name Wilson?"

"Yes," I replied. "Very much."

"So how about we call you Wilson from now on," Mr. Mbogua said.

"Yes." I was thrilled.

And so that is how I came to be called Wilson. And that is how from then on, for more than two years, at every break, when the other children of my class would run and scream, jump and dance, I sat at the back of Mr. Mbogua's class and learned English. I loved languages, how the sounds slipped off my tongue and rolled out into the world.

At night, back at Rotiken's, often sleeping underneath the stars when it was clear, I would close my eyes and say a prayer to Enkai, thanking her for my being able to learn, and then asking her to help make it last.

"Please don't let my parents forbid me from going," I would say as I set my dreams afloat into the sky. "Or let anything change the life path I am on now, which I know is so right."

"I thought you didn't approve of school," I asked Rotiken one day, as we walked the fields with his cows. I felt so uneasy, worrying that school would not last, that I wanted to know why Rotiken had had such a change of heart, given that he was the one who had told my parents and the elders to watch out for the police.

Just as I asked my question, two dik-diks ran across the path. I stopped. "Meat tonight!" I exclaimed to Rotiken, who nodded, for when two dik-diks—which are like tiny antelopes, no taller than Rotiken's knee—cross a Maasai's path, it always means there will be meat to eat.

"It isn't that I don't like school," he said, changing the subject back. Rotiken stopped and looked at the clouds, which were puffy and white like the tails of the dik-diks. "I do fear the stories of the past, and that we will lose our culture, like other African cultures have been lost, if we embrace Western ways—including school. But I think you need to go to school now. Maasai children need to learn.

"We Maasai have fallen behind," he continued, looking down and drawing lines in the cracked earth with his white cane, the colour symbolizing his position as an elder. "We are not evolving, and so we are opening ourselves up to being abused by others, including our own leaders, who have lost their way. We Maasai need to progress, to become teachers, doctors, politicians."

"I will never stop being a Maasai," I told Rotiken, thinking of some of the Kipsigis and Kikuyu children with whom I went to school, who only spoke Swahili and English, not their native tongues.

"I have seen far too many young Maasai people leave the Mara and never return," Rotiken pressed on. "They live in the big cities, now, like Nairobi, and they marry non-Maasai wives and husbands and raise their children like Western children, buying them whatever they want, and spending little time with them. I don't want that for you. You can be a great leader in the Maasai community, so you must study hard. But you alone must discover your destiny and how you juggle progress and tradition."

"I know, uncle Rotiken," I whispered. "I have felt a stirring inside me for a long time—a calling, something I am supposed to do. I am just unsure as to what it is yet. But I know school is part of my journey."

"How we evolve as Maasai, without losing ourselves, is as new to me as to you," he replied.

Halfway through our school holidays that year, uncle Rotiken took me home to visit my *papai* and *nini*. Unfortunately, their lands had become even more parched than usual during the dry season. Their concern was the cows, not my going to school. The few bushes that remained were burnt from the sun. They hadn't eaten meat since the middle of the rainy season, which was months earlier, and the milk from the cows was drying up. My older brothers were preparing to take the cows to Tanzania and asked me to come with them.

Of course, I agreed. I had my Western calendar with me and was counting down the days before I was needed back at school. I had nearly three weeks, and could travel with my brothers for that time. I folded up the paper the calendar was on and tucked it inside my *shuka*. We then prepared for our journey.

We left in the morning before the sun's rays lit up the sky. We walked and walked, as the sun rose and set, rose and set, sleeping on our blankets, which we wore around our heads by day to keep from getting heat stroke, and drinking any water we could find, and any blood and milk we could get from the cows without weakening them further.

About a week into our journey, the lands became a little more lush, with bushes that had *ormisigiyoi* flowers on them. We could even see some wildebeests heading out in front of us, which is always a good sign. Wildebeests migrate during the dry season to watering holes, and they always know where to go.

We Maasai, by the way, never eat wildebeest. For the way they hang their heads and run, they appear like crazy people. My *papai* told me when I was little: "If you eat a wildebeest, you will go mad too!"

One night, as we slept down by a river, my eyes popped open. Something had stirred, awakening me, and it wasn't a cow. I could sense that something large was near me. I became still, so still that all I could feel was my breathing. I couldn't move. The mooing of the cows eerily stopped. "A lion," I thought to myself. "A lion!"

I ever so slowly forced my body to move and inched toward my brothers Sirma and Kasaine. "Wake up," I whispered to them, shaking their shoulders. "You need to wake up. Lion…"

Instantly, at the sound of that word, Sirma and Kasaine leapt to their feet, their spears in one hand, their *congas* in the other.

Kasaine snapped at me to hide behind a tree as they slipped past the fire they had set for the night in the hopes of keeping the animals away. The dogs that had followed us were now barking wildly, and the cows' hooves were beating the ground. Sirma and Kasaine waved their spears and screamed and yelled, first in one direction and then another. But they didn't know where the lion was. So they darted back and forth as they had been trained to do.

Then I saw it, and I screamed and pointed to get my brothers' attention. The male lion was approaching the makeshift *boma* we had constructed earlier which encircled the cows near the river to keep them safe from predators. All of a sudden I heard raindrops on the ground, rain like during the wettest day of the rainy season, but it wasn't from the clouds. The cows were all peeing—a sign of their fear.

In the light from the moon and the fire, I watched Sirma and Kasaine corner the lion. Somehow they distracted the animal so much that it darted off. But then Sirma and Kasaine turned, and I screamed even louder.

Just as the elders had told me, the male lion was a decoy. Two female lions had managed to knock down a wall of the *boma*. The cows began running in every direction, knocking the other walls down. The ground shook as they moved. I stood in my place, fixed to the spot, afraid I might do something to make the situation worse, like drawing the lions' attention toward me.

The two lionesses, one after the other, dug their sharp teeth into the fleshy neck of one of the cows, as Sirma and Kasaine threw their *congas* and shouted. But the beasts were too quick. Every time a spear or *conga* was thrown, they ducked their heads down.

When the cow was dead, and drained of some of its blood, the lionesses strategically dragged the carcass off into the forest so that Sirma and Kasaine could not get at them.

I had never seen my brothers so angry...I had never seen any Maasai so angry as they were on this night. Sirma and Kasaine kicked up the dirt and threw rocks at trees, wailing their frustrations to the sky and Enkai.

All of the cows had disappeared and were roaming out somewhere on the savannah. There was nothing we could do until morning light, however, for it was too dangerous for us to venture out and look for them now. But none of us slept.

When daybreak came, we started our search. We spent that day and two more finding all the cows that had gone astray. The entire time, our shoulders were slumped and our gaits slow. In the end we had only lost two cows, but it was still the worst thing that could befall any Maasai. Our entire community would look down on us when we returned.

The night before I said goodbye to Sirma and Kasaine to head back to Rotiken's and then to school, we slept side by side by a river.

Enkai came in the form of rain. I wrapped a cowhide around me and crept underneath a big sandpaper tree to stay dry. I cried, just like Enkai was weeping. I realized I was afraid...afraid I would not become the Maasai I was meant to be. Afraid I would fail at school. Afraid that whatever stirring I was feeling inside was too big a weight for me to carry alone.

Chapter 8

Class struggle:
Jackson fights for his education

My parents, with the blessings of the elders, named me Letasuna Leteipa Ntirkana. Leteipa for being born during the night, and Letasuna after my grandfather, a great man who was known far and wide for his kindness and keen judgment. He was a quiet man, but also made children laugh, mostly by telling them stories about the animals.

"Once, this little dik-dik came across some animal poo. It tried to cross over the poo, but it got stuck. All the dik-diks from far and wide came and tried to get their friend out of the mess. But the dik-dik couldn't move. From then on, the dik-diks vowed that they would poo in neat little piles, as tall as could be, in the hopes that an elephant might one day get stuck in their poo."

When my grandfather told me this story, I laughed and laughed. And then I hugged him tight. He died before I went away to school, so I was greatly honoured to be named after him.

After I was named, I was given the raw kidney of the cow that had been slaughtered for the ceremony, which I shared with five other boys who had also just been named. We boys nibbled on our portions, while the girls ate theirs in a different part of the *manyatta*, for Maasai males and females rarely eat together at any age.

My father came and sat beside me just as I finished.

"*Papai*," I asked, "why am I given Ntirkana, your last name, and not my *nini*'s?"

"Ahh," he began, scratching his chin and looking over at the women. "The very first Maasai, the warrior who had talked with the cow, had seven wives, and each wife had her own cows. So that the wives knew which cows were theirs and which belonged to the other wives, they branded the beasts. Each wife chose a symbol that corresponded to her surname, or clan. The original Maasai people were thus made up of seven clans, with each clan a descendant from one of the original wives. Any child born became part of the clan of its mother."

"Then I should have my mother's last name?" I interjected.

"Yes, back then. But that practice changed when, one time, a cow died in its *boma*. A mother appointed her daughter to take the cows back to the field, away from the dead animal. The daughter wouldn't go, because the children had just been given a cow's kidney to eat.

"'If I go,' the daughter said, 'the others will eat it all. I won't have any.'

"The mothers all started pointing their fingers at their daughters telling them to go. None would. They all wanted to eat instead. All the other cows started to leave, because none wanted to be near the dead cow. In the end, there were no cows left. The women had lost all the cows."

"The gravest shame!" I exclaimed.

"When the Maasai men discovered this, they were very cross, of course," he said. "The men decided that from then on the clans would pass their names on from father to child, not mother to child. But one tradition does remain: all the cows continue to be branded with the symbols that represented the women's clans."

My *papai* then asked me to follow him.

We walked toward the *boma* and the cows. He opened the gate and pointed to a bull, its red head lit up by the light of the full moon. "A red-headed bull is a very prized animal," he said. "It is yours...your first bull, for your naming ceremony." He smiled at me then.

"Thank you, thank you, *papai*," I responded.

When my father left to drink local brew with the elders, I remained and stared at my bull, admiring its great muscles, which rippled under the light of the moon. At one point, our eyes seemed to look into each other's. "I think you are a very blessed cow. So I want to name you, as we only name the most special of cows," I whispered to my new friend. "I will name you Nadolukunya, 'red-headed cow."

"One day," I then thought, "when school is finished and I am an important man, I will own three hundred cows. That is my goal!"

I spent the rest of my break from school walking the sheep and learning to walk the cows alongside some of the warriors. It was a tough summer for the cows. Many got diarrhea and we had to take them to a salt-water stream a full day's walk away. Something in the saline helped their stomachs and made their skins sleek and healthy. When we travelled to the stream, we would spend as long as four days there, sleeping under the stars and letting the animals drink and graze on the grasses.

I didn't want to leave my Maasai life. But I knew the time was coming when I would have to tell my parents I would be returning to school.

"Pfft," spat my mother, when more than forty moons had passed. "You are not going to go to school, to another culture. We need you here. To be with the animals. You are a Maasai!"

In addition to my many burn scars, by this time I had several large wounds on my legs and arms from hooking, the practice in which a brother of mine would clip the end of an *ilkipirat* under my skin and then pull it out. "Look how brave I am. No one else has this many marks on their body!"

"No! No! No!" my father said, joining us. "You are not going to school. We need you to help around the *boma*. You are a Maasai! You do not need to learn what they teach in school."

"But *papai*, I want to go to school. These students at the school speak all sorts of languages and they can count. They know about the past of our country and where we are going in the future. One day," I begged, "I can—"

I stopped mid-sentence, for my mother had taken two steps forward. She was holding in her left hand an *esosian* stick, which she usually used to stir the milk in a calabash. She swatted me across the cheek so hard I lost my balance and fell over. But I didn't yell out. I'd never had a beating before, yet I knew that even the discipline of my parents was training for me to become a Maasai warrior.

My parents left me alone, to pick myself up. When I did, I tried to resign myself to the Maasai life. I slept that night on the other side of the fence from my newest friend, Nadolukunya.

But the next morning, my mother shook me awake with a surprise.

"Jonathon is here. You can go live with him. He will pay for your school books. We don't agree with what you want, but he has convinced us this school is for the best. We will let you go."

I had no idea what Jonathon had said, but I was grateful.

And so, this is how I came to live with Jonathon during the week when I went to school, and with my parents on the weekends and holidays.

Time, for me, was soon kept not by the counting of the moons, but by a calendar that I placed inside my workbook. When I was at school, I counted down the days until I was back in my *manyatta*. When I was at home, I counted down the days until I was back in my schoolhouse.

My father never mentioned school when I was with him. Our time together usually involved walking silently through the fields, listening to the love doves, tropical boubou and bush-shrikes. Occasionally, we would hear the African crow and we knew a fresh kill was near.

Often he would tell me stories about our people. One day, when we reached the yellow bark acacia tree behind which I had hidden when the Maasai policeman had come to our village, my father motioned for me to sit down. "You need to know about the Maasai," he began. I nodded for him to go on. I knew that it was important for him to tell me about our culture, our people, to balance out what I was learning at school.

"The Maasai have two delegations," he told me. "Each Maasai village—ours is made up of about six *bomas* and 157 *manyattas*—has a good delegation called an *Esiamonodolukunya* and a bad delegation called an *Esiamongiro*. For anyone who has done something wrong, like steal from another Maasai or kill, the bad delegation will determine the punishment."

There was once a person, my father told me, who killed a fellow Maasai. It was an accident. They were having a quarrel because one of the Maasai men had passed through the other's field. The man who owned the field threw his *conga* at the other man, hitting him on the head with such force that he died instantly.

The bad delegation, made up of clan elders from all the *bomas*, came together and decided that the man was guilty of murder and had to pay 250 sheep and a goat to the man's widows. "Now, we Maasai always round up our figures to nine, to represent the nine human orifices," my father told me. "So this man owed 259 sheep and nine goats."

"How did such ways come about?" I asked, thinking of how the school settled fights between students. The teachers or the headmaster usually gave detention.

"It has always been the way," he replied. "Once," he continued after a pause, "a man killed a cow. He gave the meat to all the children surrounding him. One little boy stole the kidney for himself and started to run to his *boma* with it. On the way, a crow came and tried to steal the kidney from the boy's hand. Instead, the crow killed the poor child by accident.

"The father of the boy went to the man who had given the meat to the children and demanded that he pay for the death of his son.

"'Why do I have to pay?' the man asked.

"'Because if this cow had not been slaughtered, my son would not have died.'

"The elders tried to find a middle point in the dispute because the man refused to pay for the other man's son's death. None could be found.

"Finally, the man who had killed the cow said: 'Okay. Because you told me to pay, that must mean the crow is a member of my clan. It is my brother. And I am guilty because my brother killed your son.'

"A while later, after the man who had killed the cow had paid his punishment of many cows, his own son was given the placenta of a sheep to eat. Just as he was about to bite into it, the crow swooped down and took it. The man whose son had been killed had several other sons. These boys immediately chased after the crow, swung their *congas* in the air and knocked it down. One of those *congas* killed the crow.

"The man who had originally killed the cow called a meeting with the elders. 'That crow was my brother. The father of the boys who swung the *congas* must now pay.'

"The arguments became very heated, but in the end, everyone saw the error of their ways. Whenever things happen, the Maasai settle things rationally and in discussion, or, at least, they aim to do so, not wanting to repeat the errors of the past, like what happened with the crow."

I liked this story, and I told my *papai* so. And from then on, I tried to settle all my own disputes. In football, when two players fought and I was called in to separate them, I would ask myself, what is most rational? How can I get these players to cool down and listen to one another? What would the elders do to make sure this altercation doesn't become so irrational as the one in the crow story? I knew that my *papai* wanted to make sure I followed Maasai ways, even if I was away at school.

Another time, my father told me about the seven main Maasai clans. My clan is called *Lukumai*, which means peaceful, and we settled close to Tanzania, in the southern and eastern Maasai Mara regions. Our women wear navy blue skirts underneath their *shukas*, while the women of other clans wear different-coloured skirts.

My father told me that clans from far away speak a different Maa dialect than we do. I was also forbidden, along with my brothers and sisters, to marry anyone from the *Lukumai* clan. If we are of the same clan we are considered to be related to each other. It would be like my marrying my cousin or sister.

In our community, my father also explained, the good delegation would ensure that everyone was cared for. A widow, for instance, would be supported by her oldest sons. But if a widow's husband died before her sons were old enough to support her, the delegation would step in and help. They would organize a *harambee*, in which everyone in the community would contribute what they could for the woman, such as cows, sheep, milk or fabric, to help her until her sons could take over. Or, if someone came to a *manyatta* and asked for food or help and was declined, especially by someone of the same generation, the bad delegation would punish the person and the good delegation would see that the person's needs were met.

"What happens if two Maasai are fighting?" I asked my dad once.

"Well, everyone would know," he said with a laugh, "for we Maasai are not very discreet. Everyone far and wide would gossip. But if it was serious, the elders would meet each person separately, interview them about what happened and pass their findings on to the delegation. A meeting would then be held with both parties and a positive solution would be found.

"One thing I always want you to remember," he stated to end our talk, "is that you have to respect the elders. Always talk about good things, never talk badly about other people. And whenever you find a lost cow, bring it home so a lion doesn't eat it. The owner of the cow will eventually come searching and find it."

"That's more than one thing, *papai!*"

He smiled. "We Maasai may seem quiet to the outside world, but we have a lot to say to each other!"

I enjoyed my time with my *papai*, learning about the Maasai. I also liked returning to Jonathon's *manyatta* on Sunday evenings. Jonathon didn't have children for many years after he got married. He worked as a storekeeper in the local high school, handing out textbooks. His wife, Nkoijie, considered me her own. And while I refused to become Jonathon's first son, because I didn't want to lose my own father (I would have had to renounce him), I considered him and his wife to be my second parents.

Monday mornings, I would slip off my dusty *shuka* and blanket and don my clean and crisp school uniform that Nkoijie had washed. Every time I put on the pants, I felt strange, as if my legs were being swallowed by a big snake. But I grinned and bore it.

I loved school, except for learning Swahili, which took me many years to master. The problem was that if I spoke to other students in English or Maa and a teacher overheard, I would be given a disk, which was a form of punishment. I was then to pass the disk on to any other student I heard not speaking Swahili at school—unless, of course, it was English class.

I often ended up with the disk at the end of the day because I broke into Maa more than anyone else; even if I managed to give it away, I would be given it back. I would then have to stay behind and clean the chalkboards and brushes.

My favourite subject at school was math. And I was always at the top of my class. I also used my math skills out in the Mara. When our fathers had to bring in our cattle to be sprayed with a pesticide to prevent disease, my job was to round up all the cows from *boma*s far and wide. I would run behind the animals, occasionally smacking their backsides with a big stick to make sure they followed a path right into the *olmunanta*, the narrow enclosure where the elders sprayed the animals. I then had to check the brands and count the cows that belonged to each clan. My mother's brand was like the letter U and located right over the ribs of the cows.

I would be told ahead of time how many cows each clan had sent down to be sprayed. If one was missing, I had to search for it. None of the other children could count like I could, so I was frequently called upon by my *papai* and older brothers to help them.

Despite being shy in every other class, my hand was the first in the air when the math teacher asked questions. I came away from every math course with straight As.

At school, my life was about schedules: math class at nine a.m., for instance, followed by Swahili at ten. It was also about reasoning: if I don't study, I fail. If I don't listen to my teachers, I get a detention. No one, other than the Maasai students, was superstitious—believing, for example, that Enkai will shed her tears if a sheep is slaughtered in her honour. As a result I found myself not sharing much with others about my life outside of school.

One such story began when a hyena crossed my path on the way home from school one day.

A shiver ran through me. "What bad news is to come?" I said out loud, for whenever a hyena crosses in front of a Maasai, bad luck will follow. If a black mamba snake crossed in front of me, that would be good luck. But a hyena, that greedy animal of the Mara? "No!" I gasped. These animals are so disrespected that if I ate too much food my mother would often scold: "You are greedy like a hyena!"

Seeing the hyena was not good at all. My mood was suddenly downcast. I headed straight to my mother's *manyatta*, expecting the worst, like some disease had taken hold of one of my sisters. My mother was happy when she greeted me, however, cheerfully helping my older sisters make porridge for a circumcision ceremony that was to take place the next day. I drank some *chai* and headed out to find my father, who was with the cows.

The day and evening turned out well. I fell asleep thinking to myself, "I guess this time, I avoided the fate of the hyena." My schoolmates would have thought it was nonsense to even believe in such things. Maybe they would be right.

The morning after, many of the junior warriors headed off to the circumcision ceremony. My father said I could take the cows out, all on my own. I had been accompanying him and my brothers on every holiday, for many seasons, so I knew what to do. I was excited. I called my cow, Nadolukunya, to come first and then I herded the animals out into the field.

We spent hours walking south, and all the while I sang at the top of my lungs, "*Meoshi namelong!*" "No one can beat my lovely cow."

But then, as the sun hit the midday point in the sky, my stomach started to growl. I thought of the circumcision ceremony and the porridge my *nini* had been making. I thought of the meat that would be roasting on sticks in the bush. I decided to take the cows home.

"*Papai*," I said when I saw him. "I am bringing the cows back now so I can go to the ceremony."

My father's piercing eyes said it all. No.

I spun around on my heels and took the cows back out.

I headed south again. I watched some *hadada ibis* fly overhead. I sang too, and then my stomach started to growl again. I sat down in a huff, crossed my legs and brooded. Then I returned to our *boma*, and this time I asked my mother, hoping she would have a different answer.

"Can I go to the ceremony?"

"Aren't you supposed to be with the cows?" she scolded. Her hands, face and head were now red from dye, as she was presiding over the boy's circumcision and had only just returned home before heading out again for the afternoon's food and festivities.

I shrugged my shoulders. "But everyone else is at the ceremony," I said. "Can't I go and have some meat?"

"No, we'll bring some home for you later," she said. "Your duty is to watch the cows today."

This time when I returned to the cows, my face was red and my temperature boiling. I flung a rock at a euphorbia tree, and watched the sap drip out and down to the ground. I knew the liquid was made of acid, which is exactly how I felt. Stinging mad. "I don't care if I have been forbidden to go. I'm going," I said out loud. "These cows will be fine on their own."

And so I did what no Maasai is supposed to do. I abandoned the cows. I stealthily made my way across the savannah and snuck around the back of the *boma* where the circumcision had taken place. I saw the children sitting out back, and slipped in beside them. I ate some sheep and *chapatti* and then I returned to the cows, making sure none of the men saw me.

At nightfall, I herded the cows home and acted as if I had done nothing wrong. I put them in their *boma*, then headed to my mother's *manyatta* to see if she had brought me any more meat to eat, thinking I had been with the cows the entire day.

"What are you doing there?" a man asked from the shadows of my mother's *manyatta* in a deep gruff voice.

"I'm going to sleep," I said with a big smile. "Who are you?"

The man stepped out and into the light of the moon. I saw his pockmarked face and screamed.

I started to run.

But, just like the Maasai policeman had done when I tried to get away from him, the pinching man had me. He threw me over his shoulders and paraded me back in front of my father's *manyatta*, where he stood snapping his fingers, indicating I was about to be punished.

"This boy is growing up too fast," my *papai* said to the pinching man. "He is not listening to me. I do not know what is wrong with him. Do what you need to do."

That pinching man sat down on a rock and placed me, stomach down, over his lap. He then pinched me, with his long, strong fingers and nails, all over my body, so hard I nearly screamed out in pain.

When the pinching man was done, I hobbled back to my mother's *manyatta* and told her: "I will never disobey you again. Never! Ever! I promise." And I swore I would never leave the cows again.

I also vowed to myself that I would never again question the hidden currents that move the Maasai, such as knowing that when dik-diks cross my path I will eat meat, or that seeing a hyena is a portent for trouble.

Chapter 9

Cross to bear:
Wilson and the "new" religion

My mornings in the Mara usually involved taking the sheep and then the cows into the fields, followed by a light breakfast of cow's blood and milk, and then spending the day walking the savannah with the animals. I bathed in the river, but not that often, only when I felt hot and wanted to cool down. I fell asleep under the stars, my body usually covered in dust, my muscles tired and aching from the walk.

My days at school began in the courtyard, with the ringing of the bell at eight a.m. We then had an assembly, in which we sang the Kenyan national anthem. After that, the teachers checked that we had showered and cleaned our nails. The students who hadn't were sent home, unable to return until they were clean.

During my first full year of school, I was often one of those pupils. But then I caught on and made sure to jump into the river with a bar of soap every Sunday evening and pick out the dirt from under my nails with a stick before I fell asleep.

For most of Grade 1, I was only required to be at school from Monday to Friday. But one Friday in Grade 2, late in the afternoon when my thoughts had drifted from my Swahili lessons to the weekend's activities (including having my friend Parasaloi torture me by stabbing the sharp thorns of a wait-a-bit acacia into my flesh), I discovered that school was about to become a bit more complicated.

As the other students jotted down Swahili sentences off the chalkboard, my teacher came up to me and said that I was required to be back at school on Sunday.

"Why?" I gasped. "I will be walking the cows with Parasaloi."

"All the other students, and sometimes their families, return to the school on Sunday and go to church," Mr. Frederich continued, ignoring my comment. "You know that building?" he asked, waving his hand toward the football field. "The one with the big cross on the top? That is a church."

"What is this thing called church?" I asked in Swahili.

"It's where we pray and honour God."

"Enkai…you pray to Enkai?" I asked. "I am so pleased to hear this."

"Well, I am not so sure of that, Wilson." Mr. Frederich laughed, his big stomach shaking and his smile widening. "It is where we Christians pray to God. But maybe our God is the same god as Enkai."

That following Sunday, I grudgingly arrived at school only to be whisked away by the other students to a clearing, where a man wearing a stiff navy blue suit told us to sit in a circle underneath the big yellow bark acacia tree. When we had done so, he proceeded to talk about a man named Jesus. I recognized this name. I recalled uncle Rotiken mentioning Jesus being from the land of Palestine, where it is said the Maasai are originally from.

The Maasai, according to uncle Rotiken, are one of the ten lost tribes of Israel. The story goes that the first Maasai people made their way south from Palestine in search of green pastures for their cows. They followed the River Nile through Egypt, and for a while they settled in Sudan.

But when the Maasai came into contact with the other African cultures, they became afraid. There were too many differences, not just in language, but also in their belief in one god—the other groups believed in many gods—and in how my ancestors lived their lives. The Maasai have always been nomadic, for one, meaning they never remained in the same place for long—packing up their things and rebuilding their *manyattas* along the way.

So the Maasai moved further south, past Mount Kenya, to the Maasai Mara and the Serengeti in Tanzania.

The Maasai believe that when we die, our spirits return to Enkai. We do not come back. We only have one life and the purpose of this life is to live it to the fullest, honouring Enkai in every moment and living her values.

Over the next few Sundays, at church, I learned lessons similar to those I grew up with. But the stories used to illustrate the lessons were about people named Mary and Joseph, not Maasai elders, cows, crows and hyenas.

One Sunday, after our outdoor lessons, our teacher asked us to follow him to the church with the big cross on the top. Once inside, we were told to sit cross-legged at the front and listen to a sermon by another man. When he was done, we sang songs. All the while we had to stand and then sit, sit and then stand. I was very confused. I didn't know what to do.

"Stand," he said, pulling me up by shirt. "Now sit," he would order, after a song was finished.

"Dance," he said next, after the pastor had made a few remarks.

For many weeks, I was shocked and embarrassed when I had to do this. In my *boma*, the only dancing we do is called *osikolio*, during which the junior warriors leap up and down, up and down, as high as they can. But in this place, with tall windows, I watched as the people sashayed their hips back and forth and swivelled their shoulders into all sorts of different positions as they sang along to songs in English. My body just couldn't move side to side. It could only go up and down.

I could make out some of the lyrics, though. *God created earth and heaven*, for one, and when I heard this for the first time I gasped, thinking, "This God is Enkai. She created earth and heaven. The Christian God is my god."

But when the preacher motioned for us to sit, he would speak of this God as if she was a *he*. That confused me even more. I never had time to think about it for long, though, as everyone would be up again, dancing and singing.

Sit down, stand up, sing, dance.

I became tired, so tired that I worried that by the time I made it back home I wouldn't have the energy to join Parasoloi in walking the cows.

Then, near the end of church, the pastor did something that seemed quite strange to me. He put his hand on a woman's forehead. The slim, elderly woman, wearing a hat with a long white feather out of the top, fell to the floor.

I started to rush to help her, but the boy beside me pulled me back and said, "Don't... Don't. She is supposed to do this."

The woman began talking in a language I had never, ever heard before. I swallowed hard, as her eyes darted around the room and her eyelids began to flutter. Then her tongue began to fly out of her mouth.

This preacher walked around the room and laid the palm of his right hand on some other people's foreheads, and they fell to the floor in almost the exact same way as the woman in the feathered hat had.

"Enkai, Enkai," I thought to myself, "you bring rain…but I have never seen you do this before."

Then the preacher walked up to me and slapped my forehead with such force I fell backward into the arms of two men standing behind me.

I pulled myself up and looked around. Some of the others who had been hit were rolling on the ground, still speaking this funny language.

I, however, just felt dizzy.

"I am a brave Maasai," I thought to myself. "The others couldn't stay on their feet. The purpose of this activity must be the same as allowing Parasaloi to pierce my skin. It's to toughen everyone up, so they become strong and mighty."

Many years later I learned that the church was Pentecostal and that the preacher was doing what they call the laying on of hands, in which the spirit of God was said to move through him to the parishioners. It was kind of like a blessing, I thought. I also learned that other Christian churches don't do the laying on of hands quite the same way.

Other than that, the Christians seemed to believe in much that the Maasai did. My *papai*, uncle Rotiken and other elders, for example, had shared with me the Maasai version of the Ten Commandments, starting when I was just a small child: obey your parents; no stealing; no committing of adultery; treat your neighbour the way you, yourself, wish to be treated; Enkai created earth and heaven; and the Maasai shall not love or worship any other than her.

One difference, however, was the remembering of the Sabbath, to keep it holy. We Maasai don't have a special day on which we honour Enkai. Every day is her day. She is around us, below us and above us all the time.

Since I first started attending Sunday school, every year a new church seemed to pop up in the Mara. I can recognize them because of the big wooden crosses, sometimes painted in bright colours and placed on the tops of the buildings, which stand out against the flat and sand of the Maasai Mara.

The church people seemed so foreign to me at first, with their suits and dresses and fancy hats, and especially the women, who wore blue powder on their eyelids and red paint on their lips. The church people turned out to be friendly, though, and Maasai children who attended liked the stories and the tea and cookies handed out at the end. I came to see that inside of us all there is a common thread that joins us together, no matter how different we seem.

As my uncle Rotiken told me, *taleenoi olngisoilechashur*. We are all one. Our differences are only ever external.

Chapter 10

Future tense:
Jackson learns his destiny

In my village lived an old man named Oltatuani. He was so old, the tiny holes in his ears that his mama gave him as a child had stretched down to his shoulders. His back was hunched and he had to use a cane just to shuffle his feet from his *manyatta* to the cows' *boma*. He had no teeth and his cheeks were sunken and covered in wrinkles.

But Oltatuani's eyes were bright and sparkled, especially when he told stories, as he often did, with such animation it was like he was a young man. He told stories about the five generations of Maasai that came after his birth, that's how old he was, which would have made him nearly 100 years old by the Western calendar. Oltatuani claimed to have even known the prophet Agoolonana.

Before I was named and went to school, I would see Oltatuani frequently. A close friend of mine was Oltatuani's great-great-grandson. This boy and I played *boma* together, and watched the lambs grow into sheep. When Oltatuani would see us, he would always wink and tell us he'd be right back for a story.

One time when I saw Oltatuani, however, he told me a prophecy instead, one that chilled me to the bone:

"Long ago, the wise men predicted that there would be a time in Kenya's history of great bloodshed. Tribes will turn on other tribes," he said. "That is why you have to respect yourself, and your culture, and then respect other people and their cultures, for that time has not yet come."

Then he wandered into his darkened *manyatta*.

I never saw him again.

Many moons passed and he never visited my mother. My friend, his great-great-grandson, didn't come to play with me either, which made me suspicious. Did they get malaria, or worse...typhoid? I became so concerned that one day I headed down the hill and over the savannah to their *boma*.

I was careful, though. I had had chicken pox and had to drink and wash my body in the local brew for weeks as medicine. The first time I drank the brew I became drunk, so drunk that I fell down when walking and for two days after, my head pounded. I knew not to get too close to my friend or Oltatuani in case they had a skin disease, like scabies, for I didn't want to catch it and have to drink the local brew again.

When I reached my friend's *boma*, the women were making the local brew. I could smell the aloe vera and honey in the air and I thought to myself: "They do have chicken pox!"

When I returned to my *boma*, I told my mother.

Her face became grave. "Oltatuani is not sick," she replied slowly, a tear forming in one of her eyes.

"What are you not telling me?" I asked.

"Oltatuani died. His spirit returned to Enkai. His stiff legs no longer walk this earth. The women are making the local brew for the ceremony honouring his death."

The next day, my father, some of the other men and I went to Oltatuani's *boma* and dug a big hole just outside the fence. Apparently, Oltatuani and the elders had all known that death was imminent. Oltatuani had picked out a sheep to be slaughtered for his death ceremony. It was now roasting on the fire. The women, my father told me, had used the fat from the sheep to oil Oltatuani's body to help preserve it.

At the end, all the people from his family, including his sons, grandsons and great-grandsons, had been called to his side. In the moments before he died, Oltatuani handed out all of his belongings, except his beads and *conga*, with which he would be buried. His eldest son would take possession of his *boma* and the stick he carried to indicate he was an elder. "You are now head of the family," Oltatuani had told him. "Do me proud."

The funeral ceremony commenced with the sons and grandsons standing in a line, oldest to youngest, as Oltatuani's body, wrapped by his daughters in white fabric to symbolize the spirit world, was placed in the hole that had been dug just outside his *boma*.

The elders leaned forward to examine Oltatuani's position, for if his head was crooked it would be a sign that life in his old *boma* would have some disruptions after his death. Luckily, Oltatuani's head faced straight, indicating that all would be well.

After the earth had been laid on top of him, each of the elders in attendance dropped a rock on top of the mound. At the very end, an elder sprayed some cow's milk and local brew on the mound as a blessing.

"We are still with you," the elder presiding over the ceremony said. "We will make sure your family is taken care of and loved."

Then we all ate, danced, sang and celebrated Oltatuani's long life and, of course, his stories.

"You know, son," my mother said as we walked up the hill to our *boma* at the end of the night. "A generation ago, the dead would be thrown out for the hyenas to eat."

"Yuck," I said, squishing my face up into a ball.

My mother laughed. "When our spirit returns to Enkai, nothing on earth that was once alive remains alive, so why not allow the animals to feed on our skin and bones and enjoy?" she explained. "Give them the meat from us that we have once taken from them."

"Then when did things change?" I asked.

"Christianity has changed many things. When the British came, they brought with them not only these places called schools, but also our first churches. Their spiritual leaders were not elders, but priests and missionaries. And they taught us to bury our dead so they are in one place and everyone can mourn. We agreed with this, as we had had some problems with throwing our dead to the animals. Children would often find the bones, including skulls, and bring them back home. It is not a good omen to bring a person back to their *boma*, so we started to bury our dead the Christian way."

"I heard one of the elders say that if a hyena digs up the dead body from its grave, that too is a bad omen."

"This is true, my son," my mother replied. "And another thing is true: life is a cycle...a circle."

I didn't quite understand, at least then, what my mother meant by this. But one day, I would.

In my Grade 7 year, when my studies, particularly in math, were going well, I received word at the school that I was to go home. The drought was so bad that my family, like Wilson's, was moving to Tanzania. I had to help my *papai* with the cows.

Also, like Wilson, I was devastated as I packed up my textbooks and folded my uniform, after changing back into my *shuka* and blanket. I hoped I would return to school. And if I did, I feared I would be so far behind I wouldn't catch up to my peers. The drought had gone on for so long that my father worried we would have to move away for as long as a year.

Our skins, clothes, blankets and calabashes of whatever milk the cows could deliver were tied to the backs of our donkeys. We would be walking as much as a hundred kilometres a day. I worried whether my legs were up to the task, as I had been at school, sitting in one place, for most of the year, not exercising every day by walking the cows on the savannah.

I knew I was strong from football, but not nearly as strong as the other Maasai boys of my age.

Then I became really fearful when I learned that we would be visiting the *oloiboni*, the prophet of my Maasai clan, named Oloruma, who was a descendant of the great Agoolonana.

"And you, son," my father had told me, "can come with us."

The donkeys, the children and the mamas headed south, out over the fields, toward Tanzania.

For two days, we men and boys walked southeast, instead, toward the *oloiboni*.

I breathed into any cramps I felt in my body from lack of exercise. And braved the calluses that formed on the soles of my feet from walking barefoot.

Everyone suffered from fatigue, wanting to collapse under the weight of their bodies but forcing themselves to press on, under the scorching heat of the midday sun. Even the nights were hot and humid as we neared the ocean. I had never felt humidity on my body and it itched.

When we finally arrived at the place, more than a hundred other Maasai had already set up *boma*s for their cows out in the fields of the savannah.

"*Opayia lenye*," my *papai* said to a Maasai elder who had a vacant piece of land beside his cows' *boma*. "My friend."

"*Kanjiengua?*" the elder asked. "Where are you from?"

"Way over that mountain, where the sun comes up. Near Mount Kokaa," my father replied, motioning with his hand in the direction from which we came. "The grasses are very dry and we don't have any water for the cows or for ourselves."

"How many are you? How many cows did you come with?" the elder asked.

"The women have gone on. There are six of us, here, 76 cows and 52 sheep and goats."

"I am from the family Ilasser," the elder said.

My dad smiled. "So am I."

"We are brothers, then," said the elder, nodding his head and smiling. "Please set up your *boma* near my own and let my sons help you."

And that is how the conversation went all the way down to Tanzania and back when we met other Maasai families. Everyone, somehow, is family.

I learned that the Osupuko part of Kenya's Maasai Mara, where the *oloiboni* lived, was lush. It was located in between several mountains, and until the *oloiboni* settled there, no one had dared set up their *boma*s in the area, for fear that the land, covered in bushes and forests, was full of lions. Even when the land was cleared and some of the wives began planting gardens of vegetables, having purchased seedlings from Kipsigis tribeswomen at markets, there was fear that the lions would attack.

"But the land is good, very good," explained the elder who let us set up camp near him. "This area gets lots of rain. It would be good if all of the Mara was like this," he then said, waving his hand over the lush valley below us. "The cows and other livestock would not go hungry, and we would broaden our diets with the vegetables and grains we could plant here."

My father nodded in agreement, but we both knew that moving here was impossible. Our entire family, for several generations, had settled in the Naikarra area. Besides, if all the Maasai moved to this fertile part of the Mara, it would become overcrowded. And then no one would benefit.

That night, as the children began to sing, my father nudged my elbow. "It is time. The *oloiboni* has asked to see all of the elders from in and around Naikarra. We are to go to his hut. There is one other boy coming, the son of Rureto."

"Wilson," I gasped. "I didn't know he would be here."

"Is he your friend?" my father asked.

"Yes," I replied with a smile, not feeling so alone anymore among all the men.

Despite it being cooler in the valley than on the savannah, the stone and mud hut was hot from the fires, so I took off my blanket and held it in my hand as I sat cross-legged on the floor, across from Wilson.

He was nervous, like me. I could tell from his perspiring forehead and his hands, which he wrung together.

For a brief moment our eyes locked, and I knew what he was thinking, for I was thinking the same: "What if the *oloiboni* doesn't like me?"

When the *oloiboni* held his long cane out to me, I swallowed hard, thinking this was the moment when he would tell me to leave. I took the end and squeezed. He merely nodded and his gaze turned elsewhere. I breathed a sigh of relief. This was a sign that I was accepted.

"And you," he then said, pointing his walking stick at Wilson. I jumped, as Wilson's eyes popped open.

"And you," he repeated, "will one day work with the white people. You will bring our story of the Maasai to people in the West. You will be our bridge. The bridge of your generation to the world."

I exhaled. Wilson wasn't asked to leave. None of us were.

"And you," he said, pointing to a young man, whom I knew was named Darius—he attended my school, but we had never been in the same class.

"And you," the *oloiboni* said a second time to Darius, "will be a very important person in the community."

"And you," he then said, as his trance-like gaze, made even more penetrating by the white circles he had drawn around his eyes, fell on me. "And you will help them both."

The next morning, as the sun rose over the mountains, on the other side of which was the ocean, a fish eagle flew over me. It showed me its white underbelly, and that meant I would have good food to eat that day.

I stretched my arms up over my head and thrust my own stomach out, as a way of saying thank you to the bird and to Enkai, who had sent me this blessing.

I recalled what the *oloiboni* had said at the end of his prophecy the night before. "Good things are coming to all of us," he had pronounced. "There will be some struggle, but in the end, much change and success will arrive."

The fish eagle, and the *chapatti* and *chai* the *oloiboni*'s wives made me for breakfast, were signs that change was indeed in the air.

Chapter 11

Caving in:
Wilson and the rites of passage

My grandfather was a very wise man, just like his son, Rotiken. When I was little and my grandfather was still alive, we children would sit around the fire and he would tell us stories. He would always start his stories slowly and then speed up, piercing the sharp end of his spear into the ground whenever he got excited or mad.

More than anything, he liked to tell stories about a giant named Olarinkoi.

"This Maasai giant," my grandfather would begin, "was the first warrior to go into the cave." But Olarinkoi was not a kind giant. He terrorized Maasai communities far and wide. He stole their cows and demanded that the Maasai be at his beck and call. No one could challenge him because he was so big, so fierce, and he lived far up a hill, in a cave as deep as the Mara River.

Now, this giant ordered everyone around. And one of his first commands was that the community below light a fire in the middle of the river.

The elders in the village looked at each other in awe. "How do we set a river on fire?" they asked.

A Maasai boy, just past another important landmark or initiation, his second naming ceremony followed immediately by his circumcision, knew what to do. He told the elders to place a bird's nest in the middle of the river and set it ablaze just when the giant begins to head down the mountain. The elders did so, and when the giant saw it, he was impressed.

"Now I want a handful of fleas," he bellowed to the elders. "Put them in your hands and bring them to me."

"But the fleas will all jump out. This is an impossible task!" the elders told each other.

They went to the boy, who told them to find a donkey. "Cut the mane of the donkey into pieces with a machete and place the pieces in your hands. When the giant arrives, open your hands. The wind will blow the pieces away, but they will look like fleas and at least you can say, you had the fleas for him."

The elders did that and the giant was again impressed.

The giant then asked for a toothbrush made out of metal. "This is very difficult, impossible!" they told the boy, who smiled.

"Tell the giant he will have his toothbrush, but we need a year to make it," the boy replied.

The giant agreed, but he said every day until the toothbrush was ready, he wanted a calabash of fresh milk to drink.

The Maasai elders looked at each other. "What can we do? It is too far to keep bringing this giant milk to his cave every day." But the giant threatened to kill all the Maasai mamas if he didn't get his milk.

The elders went to the boy, who was by this time turning into a young man. He said to tie the mouth of a cow together so it wouldn't moo and take it up the mountain. He would go up the mountain and stay there, milking the cow every day and delivering the giant his milk.

The young man lived up on the mountain in a cave not far from the giant's. Every day, he left a fresh calabash of milk in front of the giant's cave. And every second or third day, someone trudged up the mountain and gave the young man fresh meat to eat and cow's blood to drink.

The rainy season passed into dry, and then back to rainy again. All the while, the young Maasai man ate and ate, and built up his strength by running up and down the mountain, carrying boulders on his back. He practiced throwing his spear against trees. And, in his spare time, he prayed to Enkai. He himself grew into a giant—a peaceful giant, who honoured the true path of the Maasai and their God.

One day, an elder visited the young man and said: "We are depending on you to kill the giant. You are now as strong and as big as him."

"I will do it!" replied the young Maasai man.

The Maasai elders convened a meeting. They asked the giant to join them. Olarinkoi thundered down the hill, shaking the yellow bark acacia trees with every step.

When everyone had gathered together in a circle, a Maasai elder announced to the giant: "We have made your metal toothbrush. And the person who made it is here with us today."

The young man stepped forward. "Thank you very much for this meeting today. And thank you very much for the cow's blood and meat that was given to me. I am now very strong." And he heaved his *conga* high into the air and smashed it down on the giant's head, killing him instantly.

The story doesn't end there. The young man, the very first Maasai to head to the cave, was so shocked the ruse worked that he died instantly, on the spot.

I remember a sense of sadness overtaking me when I first heard this story.

For many, many generations, Maasai boys have headed to caves shortly after their circumcisions. The cave they go to is decided upon by elders; it is usually located within the region where a number of boys of the same generation live. The young men can spend many months, often years, in the cave living alongside as many as a hundred other male youth, learning Maasai traditions and stories, making medicines and training physically to slay lions.

Slaying a lion has marked a Maasai male's shift from childhood into manhood. I wanted the origins of this tradition to end with a victor who lived long into the future. Instead, I was left wondering about what the first Maasai warrior's life would have been like if he had lived. Then my thoughts turned to what the cave might offer me.

"So what is it like?" I asked my friend Terugee, when he emerged after spending nearly two years straight in the cave.

Terugee had long been named when Jackson, Darius and I came into the world (meaning, in Western time, he was about a decade older than all of us). He was born at the beginning of our generation, Jackson and I nearer to the end.

Terugee, who had never set foot in a school and came from a village very close to the prophet's own *boma*, headed into the cave right after his circumcision. Except for two long stretches during which he travelled with his family's cows to Tanzania, Terugee had been in the cave for nearly six years, he thought, based on the passing of the seasons that had elapsed.

Finally, he had completed his task. He killed a lion. And the four of us were out in the savannah, watching some cows, the morning after the big celebration to honour Terugee's kill. Terugee, still wearing the lion's mane from the beast he had felled, sewn into a headdress by his mother, was smiling and lethargic after all he had experienced.

"Yes, tell us, tell us, please," urged Darius, tilting his head to the side and squinting his eyes in the sun. Jackson, Darius and I had become close since we formally met in the *oloiboni's manyatta.*

"Well," Terugee began, drawing out his words, "it all began after I was shaved and had my circumcision ceremony, during which my name was blessed for the second time. After the circumcision, I was dressed in a blue *shuka* and a headdress made out of white beads with an elephant ivory broach in the front. I then waited, and the moon waned from full to half before my father entered my mother's *manyatta*, where I was resting, and gave me a solid steel spear, the handle of which was made from white bush. The end was so sharp that I pricked my finger on it. He also gave me a *conga* made out of the finest *Olea Africana* wood, a horn made out of cow skin and a bell."

"I know what the bell is for," I chimed in. "It is to alert our families of prey coming toward the *boma*. It is also for calling the lion. Once the lion hears the bell, the bravest and fiercest of all will leave the safety of the big leaves under which it spends its days and willingly come to meet its death."

"So true," Terugee agreed. "It will not be an easy battle," he then added, after a long pause in which his eyes scanned the savannah. "And the victor may not be you. Many Maasai young men have been killed by the lion, for not being ready for the chase. But when you are ready, you will know, and that lion will come to the sound of your bell."

"And when you kill it, it will be with you for the rest of your life. Its spirit will be entwined with your own," Darius interjected, and then, more shyly, added: "The elders told me."

"How did your journey to the cave begin?" Jackson asked.

"After my father gave me those things, my uncle arrived and asked me to come with him," Terugee said. "When we were standing in the cows' *boma*, he pointed to a big black bull. 'This is for you to take to the cave when it is your turn to contribute the meat,' my uncle said, patting me on the shoulder.

"My father, my uncle and I then slept under the stars. Before the sun rose, we began our trek to the prophet's *boma*. While little was said between my father, my uncle and me, the silence spoke a great deal. I was soon to be one of them."

"What happened next? At the *oloiboni's*?" I asked, trying to be as patient as I could.

Wilson and Isaac in class.

Wilson, Mungasio and Kasaine playing football in the Maasai Mara.

Simon, Oloshorua and Wilson on a field trip to Nairobi.

Jackson and Edward at Naikarra Secondary School.

Wilson and Benson learn about planes on a field trip.

Wilson and Philip at a music festival in Narok.

Jackson with his uncle Jonathon making soup in the cave.

Wilson and Jackson hanging out at Rotiken's home.

Wilson and Lenkoko participating in a music festival.

The Naikarra Boys Choir, and Wilson crouching in the middle.

Jackson outside of his brother's home.

Jackson looks out over his community in Naikarra.

Wilson and Jackson are greeted by Free The Children staff in Canada.

Wilson and Jackson support the Toronto Maple Leafs at their first hockey game.

Wilson and Jackson meeting Former Vice President Al Gore.

Wilson and Jackson chat with Martin Sheen.

Jackson in a Free The Children classroom.

Wilson and Jackson outside of a classroom in Naikarra.

Wilson takes a second to pose.

Jackson outside of an old mill in Emori Joi.

Jackson with an international volunteer at Me to We's Bogani Cottages.

Wilson in his doorway at home.

Jackson, a local hero in his community, surrounded by children.

Wilson and Jackson watching the cattle in Maasailand.

Wilson teaches guests how to throw a rungu.

Jackson teaching how to use a bow and arrow for weapons training.

Wilson with his mama.

Jackson with his mama and brother.

Wilson and Jackson at a ceremony in Sikirar.

Wilson and Jackson hanging out.

V. Tony Hauser

Wilson, the stoic warrior.

V. Tony Hauser

Jackson and that charming smile.

"The *oloiboni* spent much time with the elders, including my father, while I waited outside with eight other young men. When our fathers and uncles emerged from his *manyatta*, the prophet asked to see us. Once my eyes eventually adjusted to the dull light inside his hut, I saw nine small wooden stools laid out in a semicircle in front of the *oloiboni's*, who was sipping local brew, and whose face had already been decorated in white chalk. The nine of us were asked to each take a stool.

"All of our eyes were glued to the prophet, who began to sing a song about a young warrior heading to a cave to meet the lion. As he did so, he drew lines on our forehead and cheeks. '*A blessing, a blessing*,' he sang, '*for the boys soon to become men*.'

"'I have chosen all nine of you,' he eventually said, 'because you each have qualities that will help the others in the cave. Like the forest, one will act as a tree and anchor the birds that fly around it, the worms that feed on it and the lions that sleep underneath. One will be the rain that provides nourishment. Another will be the sun.'

"The *oloiboni* then sang that he had recognized in a prophecy that I would excel as the scout, going first to hunt our prey and, during raids, to identify the best places to steal cows.

"When he was done singing our duties, we left the prophet, said gruff and manly goodbyes to our uncles and fathers and followed a senior elder as he led us to the cave we would call home—with as many as one hundred other boys on some nights."

As Terugee sipped some milk from his calabash, I pictured him in the cave. In my mind's eye, I could see him underneath the stone outcropping, his ears alert to the sound of lions moving in the thick bushes, his eyes darting at every movement. He would indeed have made a good scout.

"That very first day, the nine of us killed a bull," Terugee said suddenly, jarring me from my reverie. "We skinned it, roasted it and then ate the ribs first, licking all the juices and smacking our lips together when done. We then walked around the cave and gave the other young men, all placed in groups of nine as well, pieces of meat. The others had been in this cave (or another) for many, many moons. All nine of us felt a little intimidated, but we dared not show our fear. I puffed up my chest and acted like I had been in the cave as long as anybody.

"That very first night, with our bellies full, we fell asleep to the cries of the bush babies, our backs prone on the hard rock floor of the cave, the walls echoing with every cough and snore.

"The very next day unfolded like many to come. We woke early, drank some milk and cow's blood, and then divided our chores between the nine of us. Collecting firewood, making our bedding and fetching water from the stream at the bottom of the hill were just some of the tasks I was frequently assigned.

"All the while a senior elder looked on, his eyes peering down his long, thin nose, watching us and assessing how we communicated with each other and how dutifully we completed our tasks.

"After performing our chores, we would sharpen our spears using rocks that we held tightly between the thighs of our legs. We spent many afternoons collecting herbs to make into medicines, including soups, which our mamas had been teaching us how to do since we were small children. Most of these herbs we kept in a dry place in the cave in case any of us got ill. But some of those herbs—particularly pieces of *Olea Africana*, which we would heat—we mixed in with our morning and evening cow's blood and milk, for it was said that these medicines would make us strong."

As Terugee spoke, I thought of my own mama, who had been teaching me how to make these same medicines almost since I could walk.

"Every third or fourth moon, before the sun hit the midday point of the sky, two of us would head down the mountain to fetch milk from the village mamas below," Terugee continued. "The mamas in the *boma* below were always waiting for us, with calabashes spilling over with fresh milk. Every night we had meat, from either one of our own bulls or a bull brought by another young man in the cave. And stories, from the elders who came up to join us. Stories about the giant, the first Maasai warrior to live in a cave; stories about how we are to settle disputes with one another; stories about how to be a good Maasai, to listen, to not fight with one another. Stories about always being peaceful."

I began reciting one of Rotiken's stories, one he had first shared with a group of initiates in the cave: "Long, long ago, there was a lion who was so demanding, like Olarinkoi was to the Maasai, that every animal in his kingdom responded to his beck and call, out of fear. Every few nights, the lion called a meeting of all his species and said things like: 'Mr. Antelope, you are my food today.' And then the lion would eat him. In another meeting, the lion said to the wildebeest, 'You are my food today.' And then the lion ate him.

"This went on and on and on, until there were no animals left except the tortoise. When the lion told the tortoise that he would be the food, he replied, in the bravest voice he could muster, 'But I am a cripple. I carry cement on my back. It is shameful for you to eat me. I am not fast. I am too easy.'

"The lion thought about what the tortoise had said but didn't care. 'I'm going to eat you anyway.'

"The tortoise replied, 'Okay, but first take me to the river. When I am wet, my shell is softer.' When they reached the river, heavy rains came and the tortoise managed to slip into the water when the lion was blinded by wind. The tortoise escaped the lion by hiding in a dam.

"The moral of this story is that even the weakest among us, or so we may think by their appearance, may be the strongest of all."

"Kind of like me," Jackson piped up.

I laughed. He was right. "Yes, kind of like you," I replied.

Terugee then told the three of us what it was like to go on his first raid. A long time ago, going on a raid meant the warrior was brave, and brought honour to his family. If the warrior was successful and brought back a cow or cows, he added to his family's wealth and showed other families that he was a hardworking son. Back then, going on a raid was seen as the right thing to do in our culture.

"Even though it was still daylight," Terugee began, "I had been sleeping, knowing that I would be awake the entire time the moon would be in the sky. I had been in the cave now for nearly one full circle of the sun and moon, a Western year. The nine of us and the elder entrusted with being our guide decided we were prepared. We could go on our first raid. We had walked up and down the mountain with boulders on our backs so many times that the muscles in our legs and backs bulged. We had sat in on so many discussions with the older boys that we knew how to settle disputes.

"Since I had been designated by the prophet as the scout, I had to go first, identify the Kipsigis farm from which we would steal cows and then report my findings to the others.

"I changed into my red *shuka* and a blanket that I had purposely covered in mud to camouflage me, and tied to my body four calabashes of milk to sustain myself. I then made my way down the mountain, alone, breathing in the cool air of the start of the wet season. My leather sandals, which I had made one afternoon in the cave, protected my feet from the thorns.

"When night came, I followed the light of the moon. I walked and walked, knowing that at sun up, the others would follow my tracks.

"When night cloaked me for a second time, the Maasai Mara began to leave me. The grasses under my shoes began to get shorter and shorter, having been cut for crops. I scratched my arms at one point while making my way through cornfields that had failed to yield, because of the lack of rain. When morning came, my footsteps became lighter and my body shrunk into itself as I stealthily moved onto Kipsigis land, my ears alert to the sound of their cows' bells.

"When I finally saw a herd out grazing, I crept my way over the earth until I was safely hidden behind some bushes.

"I remained hidden, watching the Kipsigis men and women conduct their chores, until the sun set. I knew I needed to identify a hut where the men appeared frail and where there were no young men.

"When I finally snuck out from hiding, I pretended I was tracking a buffalo, just in case anyone saw me, by raising my spear high in the air and keeping my eyes glued to the ground. When I finally identified the best hut to raid, I spent that entire night heading back. I met my eight peers, who were waiting for me, just over a mountain, well into Maasailand.

"I slept as the others planned the raid, which would take place during the darkest part of the night, just before the rooster calls."

I sighed and shook my head as Terugee stopped to take another drink. I breathed in and out steadily as I was out of breath from just listening to him. "You leave us all in suspense," I finally said. "Please finish the story."

"We then travelled to the Kipsigis home I had identified," Terugee jumped right back in. "We crept up on the cows, undid a big black bull's bell so it would no longer ring and slipped a rough rope around the bull's neck. We did this for two other bulls as well and then made our way back to the Mara. No one saw us. There was no fight. There was no death."

I exhaled. "Thank goodness," I whispered.

"It was fortunate," Terugee said. "The Maasai rarely take Kipsigis cows anymore, so they likely weren't expecting us. We slaughtered the bulls and shared the meat with the others in the cave.

"After that, we went on two more raids, the nine of us, and each time we returned safely, having had no Kipsigis cross our path. We came to be known as the best raiders in the cave, and everyone urged us to go whenever meat became scarce. We saw these cows that we took from our raids as a blessing. We had done what our forefathers had done." Terugee paused to let their achievement sink in. We all knew that successful raids were among the most important of young warriors' tasks.

"After that first raid, we stepped up our preparations for killing the lion," Terugee said a few moments later, his story-telling now coming faster. "We started by tracking and killing buffalo. These are big, wild beasts, whose footsteps I, in particular, would sometimes have to track for days. I had to be very careful, for elephants were often near, plus buffalo can smell humans, or so the senior elders had told me in the cave. I always had to be downwind from the big creatures, for they would charge me and possibly kill me, with the force of their weight, if they smelled me near.

"The elder in the cave taught me how to keep my scent behind any animal, by tossing strands of grass in the air to determine which direction the wind was blowing. When I had a buffalo within sight, I contacted the others by blowing the horn, and then we attacked, like we would a lion, dancing from foot to foot, not peering at the creature in the eye, and then thrusting our spears into its hard skin. The first few times, we were so weak that our spears barely broke through the animal's hide. But soon enough, we were killing the creatures with only a few blows. In total we killed ten buffalo…and this was before we were even ready to start hunting lions.

"It was a magical time," Terugee said. "At night, I learned from the elders that every Maasai has a different character. Some are cool and calm, others fiery and temperamental. The elders taught me how to listen to people, to feel their energy before imposing my own. That's how to communicate properly. 'Always be respectful,' one elder told me. 'Listen before you speak.'

"By day, we made ourselves stronger. We chased after the swift and speedy antelopes to strengthen our legs and gain our own speed. The faster and smaller the creatures, the quicker we became. With the dik-diks, we had to navigate the bushes, learn how to run at top speed over boulders and to leap rivers, and then how to throw our spears with such precision as to hit their hearts, often while the creatures were still on the run themselves.

"Then, we were ready to slay a lion. All nine of us. The elder told us one night after we had eaten our cow. And, of course, I was sent out first, as the scout, to find them."

"Tell, tell," I said, leaping up and down with excitement. "Tell us how you killed the lion."

"Well," he started, after a long pause. "That is something I can't share. Only you can experience that for yourself. But I *can* tell you another story," he said, knowing that Darius, Jackson and I felt cheated out of the full tale. "One that tells of why I cannot say more.

"Way back, before the Maasai killed lions, there was a warrior. He was hungry and went into the forest alone to kill animals and eat their meat. When he emerged and told the others what he had done, they were in shock. 'Lions live in there!' they exclaimed. 'How do you survive them? Kill one for us, for lions are carnivorous and our truest enemy.'

"'Okay,' replied the warrior. 'I will go back into the forest and chase the animals out. Anything and everything you see, you can kill. But tell me, before I go, how big is this lion?'

"One of the warriors spread open his arms as far as they would stretch. 'This big,' he said.

"'I can do that!' replied the first warrior. And so he went into the forest. Day passed and there was no sound. Then, when night had fallen, the warriors standing just outside the forest heard a big commotion: hoofbeats shaking the rough earth, birds cawing, the rustling of leaves.

"They held up their machetes and *congas* and killed the animals one by one as they emerged.

"But in the end, there were no lions.

"When the warrior came out of the forest, the other warriors were stunned, for around his neck was the skin of a lion. 'I wrestled it to the ground with my own hands,' he boasted to his friends. 'It was nothing for me.'

"The other warriors all wanted to know how he did it. But the brave warrior said the only way for them to really learn how to kill a lion was to kill one on their own."

I couldn't wait for that opportunity. I had spent my life, since I could talk and understand others, preparing for the moment when I would face the lion. A chill ran through me when I imagined it. Would I be confident or afraid? Would my spear kill or miss? Only time would tell.

Chapter 12

Cuts like a knife: Jackson and the sharp end of tradition

When I was in Tanzania with my family, my *papai* told me a different version of how the giant in the cave met his death. It involved a beautiful young woman. When Olarinkoi began terrorizing the Maasai, the elders decided to send a young woman to the giant's cave. She went by herself and, at first, hid in a darkened corner. From there she studied how the giant ate his meat and drank his blood.

She thought she had gone unnoticed, but the next day, without saying a word, the giant threw some meat to the young woman. He didn't say hello. He didn't ask her name. He just threw her some food, which she ate. The young woman decided afterwards to move a little closer to the fire, to warm her chilled body.

Every day, the giant left in the morning and returned at nightfall, roasting his meat and giving the young woman her share. He said nothing to her. She said nothing to him. And every day, she kept moving a little closer, until eventually she was in his bed. "Where are you from?" he finally asked her.

She replied: "I am from nowhere."

"What caused you to come here?

"I decided to join you because I do not know where I am."

The young woman was very beautiful, so the giant tried to be nice. However, every time he left in the morning to go hunting, the young woman slipped down the mountain and relayed to the elders all that she had seen and talked about with the giant. The young woman told the elders, for instance, that the giant does not nap, but there was a part of the night when he slept so soundly, nothing could wake him, not even the young woman's soft touch.

That next night, the young woman had the giant stay up much later than he usually did, telling her stories. He was eventually so tired that he passed out. The young woman once again slipped down the mountain, and told the elders the giant was asleep. A group of Maasai warriors raced up the mountain and hit the giant over his head with their *congas*. The giant died.

While there are different versions of the origins of the Maasai cave tradition, the meaning remains the same: in the face of adversity, there is always an answer, and we can slay even the most ferocious and fearsome of our foes.

When I returned from Tanzania with the cows, after being gone for about a Western year, I went back to school. My father said he was proud of me for abandoning my classes to be with the Maasai. "You have shown you are worthy and can balance both of your lives," he said with a twinkle in his eye. "So this is what I would like you to do. You go to school and write those examinations to go to high school—"

I gasped. "How do you know about high school?"

"Jonathon told me," he replied, placing a warm hand on my shoulder. We were standing by the cows' *boma* on a starlit, clear night, the rains having at last washed and watered the land where I was born.

While we were away in Tanzania, my father explained, he heard of a strategy some of the other Maasai families were using during the drought. The Maasai men were taking just one wife with them on the journey, leaving their other wives, the older girls and the youngest children back on the Mara.

In times of drought, the exodus to Tanzania often resulted in the death of small children due to malnutrition and diseases like typhoid. "Leaving the other wives and older daughters at home to care for the small children would enable us to move more quickly to Tanzania," my father continued. "We could then sell some of the cows and milk in markets as we travel to the Serengeti, and then send the money home, which the women could use in Naikarra or Narok to buy their own milk, vegetables, fruits and rice.

"Kipsigis food, I know!" my *papai* exclaimed. "But it got me thinking. It was a father who had gone to school, who came up with this idea. And it works. So I thought we could take an old custom and modernize it to help you, for maybe if you are educated, you can help us all."

I looked into my *papai*'s brown eyes. He had lost three children—three of my own siblings—due to disease, including two while en route to Tanzania. He was tired. He clearly couldn't hang on to just the old ways anymore.

"But there is one condition," he said, as I tried to contain my excitement. "You must kill the lion first."

I was not as far behind in school as I thought I would be after nearly a year's absence. One thing I had in my favour was that whenever I could, while travelling, I would do math equations using a long stick in the sand. I took two books with me to Tanzania, too—an atlas, in English, and *Intepen E Maasai* by S.S. Ole Sankan, a book about the Maasai people—both of which I read and re-read. They were small books I could tuck into the back of the beaded belt I wore around my *shuka*. Reading these whenever I was out with the cows helped me keep up with my languages.

My teacher did a small test when I came back to school at what would have been the start of my Grade 8 year. Based on my results, he said my peers were ahead, but I could easily catch up. I wouldn't have to repeat the grade. I was relieved and began to study even harder, knowing I would be writing the national examinations at the end of the last school term.

By the time our winter break came in July, I had regained my position at the top of the class in math and science, and near the top in my other subjects. I left for my holidays nervous about the national examinations scheduled for November, but confident I would get a placement in a high school.

"Son," my father began one night, sitting down beside me. In front of us was a raging fire, and I was roasting some corn on a metal tray. We Maasai never had corn until we started leaving our mamas behind on our treks to Tanzania and they bought the kernels at the market. Roasted corn had become one of my favourite foods.

I looked up. My mother stood behind my father, so I knew what he wanted to tell me was serious. My mother and father never had conversations with me together, unless it involved the pinching man or making decisions concerning my life, like about school.

"If you do well on these national exams," he began, "you can go to high school. I promised. But you still need to be a warrior. It is time," he then said, lowering his head and drawing lines in the sand with his spear. "It is time that you are circumcised and head to the cave."

"But *papai*," I whispered, swallowing hard, hoping the tears that were welling in my eyes would be sent back down with the motion. "I write the exams in a few months. I won't have time to go to the cave."

"You might. If you show you are worthy and slay the lion by the time of the exams, then you can write them."

"But I have to go to school before the exams. I can't miss school, or else I will be behind and fail the exams."

I anxiously thought of Terugee, and having to spend six years in the cave like him. He had breaks during those six years, but I knew my schooling would end permanently if I had to spend that much time in the cave.

I refused, however, to show my *papai* my fears.

My father and I remained quiet as we thought about the predicament.

"I think you just need to trust," my mother said, stepping forward. "Trust Enkai and trust your own spirit that is connected to her, that what is meant to be, is meant to be."

"Yes," my father continued. "Your mother is right. I will support you in your efforts to continue with school, if you support me and make yourself into the finest warrior first."

Over the next few days, my mother and the other women in the *boma*, including my older brothers' wives, prepared for my circumcision ceremony. As I watched them head out into the savannah to pick the aloe vera for the local brew, my mind tossed and turned over what I was going to do. I couldn't miss school. If I did, so close to the exams, I would definitely not do well. But I could not defy my father. I knew he had been more accepting of my decision to go to school than most Maasai fathers. In fact, the few other fathers in Naikarra who let their children attend school pulled them out at the end of Grade 8, if not earlier. Some children never went back after their migrations to Tanzania. Others attended only when the police took them. If I did well and was accepted into high school, I would be the first of anyone in any *boma* far and wide to actually go.

My mind was still churning the day before my circumcision, when I was woken early and told to bathe in the river with a brand new bar of soap. When I was done, my brothers, waiting by the bank of the river, took my old dusty red *shuka* and blanket and helped me put on a royal blue *shuka*. I also wore a pair of brown leather sandals that one of my brothers made for me.

Heading back to the *boma*, I met my mother at the gate. She placed a headdress made of white and yellow beads over my head. She then placed a new necklace, triangular in shape, also of white and yellow beads, around my neck. Then I was told to relax on my mother's bed, which was made up with fresh *lantana camara* leaves.

As my sisters made *chapatti*, my brothers wandered into the *manyatta*, one after the other, and told me stories about their circumcision and cave experiences.

"For a moment, our eyes locked," my brother said, surprising me by revealing information about his time with the lion.

"I became still, so still, fearing I had alerted the lion to my intentions. His golden eyes seemed to look right through me, into the depths of my soul. I thought he was going to lunge. I thought I was a dead warrior. Then he looked away so suddenly that a force deep within me lifted my arm and I threw my spear with a strength I didn't know I had, killing him with one blow."

"Wow," I exclaimed.

"Just remember not to wince when you are circumcised," he then advised. "If you do, you will bring so much shame to our family. No girl will marry you. And no girl will want to marry the brother of someone who flinched. Everything you have done in your life has prepared you for this moment."

I gulped.

I could do this, I knew, although I wasn't really concentrating on my circumcision at all.

Instead, I was thinking about how I was going to slay the lion in just shy of six weeks.

At some point in the mid-afternoon I headed out to the savannah with my mother in front of me and the mama who would preside over the circumcision ceremony behind me. We went in search of *ormisigiyoi* flowers, which the women would attach to the calabash of fresh milk used in the ceremony.

On our way back, my father and brothers were bringing in the cows. They stood in a line and watched, for if the cows went straight into their *boma*, with no wavering, it was a good omen that I would not flinch. If they dawdled or left the line to munch on some grasses, it was a bad omen.

I held my breath as I followed my mother to her *manyatta*, learning only later that evening that the cows went straight. "You received a blessing today," my father said, beaming, as we sat together. "Enkai is watching you."

Before daybreak, my mother shook my shoulder and told me to rise. My eyes were fuzzy. But I forced myself awake, knowing that this was perhaps the most important day of my life.

The *oltoroboni*, the man who would do my circumcision, had arrived the day before, but I had not yet met him. He was Maasai but he didn't keep livestock. He killed animals as a hunter-gatherer, and, as a result, knew how to perform intricate cuts and surgeries with precision.

He practised circumcisions on zebras, I was told.

After the *oltoroboni* arrived, my family cleaned everything in the *boma* with soap and water, washing all the evil spirits away. He sharpened his knives with crystal and ate goat meat and drank milk with cow's blood.

The *oltoroboni* always arrived the day before the actual circumcision and did little things the elders and family would watch to ensure he performed the circumcision fairly. You see, his goal was to make me flinch by using a dull knife or putting pepper on the blade so it would sting my skin. My brothers stood over him as he readied his blade, watching his every move to make sure the knife was sharp.

My father, two elders and my father's eldest son finally entered the *manyatta*, along with the *oltoroboni*, who was wearing a *shuka* made out of cow skin dyed black. When the *oltoroboni* drew his knife, I studied the silver blade, which glittered in the light from the fire.

The *oltoroboni* said nothing the entire time he cut away at my foreskin. I felt the pain ricochet up my spine and down my legs, but I remained rigid, showing no discomfort.

When we were done, and I was wearing a thick bandage made out of fabric, I was given as much milk to drink as I wanted. I was told to lie on the bed of fresh *lantana camara* leaves for as long as I needed to rest, while the mamas outside decorated the clay walls with *Olea Africana* leaves, indicating to all the guests that this was where the circumcised boy, who did not flinch, lived.

Over the next week, as I recovered from my circumcision, my *papai*, *nini* and other relatives gave me ten cows for my bravery, including a big black bull with a white spot on its belly from my father. "It is the best cow of all," my *papai* stated with pride. "For a great son."

Then, after several moons had passed, some of the junior warriors from other *boma*s approached my father.

It was early morning, the sun having just reached the peak of the mountain to the east. "We would like to take your son, Letasuna Ole Ntirkana, now," they said, in soft, hushed voices one after the other.

The junior warriors, who had all completed their cave duties, sat on the ground, huddled together with my father for what seemed like ages, until *papai* eventually stood up. He came over to where I was sitting, patiently waiting, on a wooden bench.

"It's time," he said, his tone serious. "You will start the walk to the *oloiboni* today, and then you will be taken to the cave."

Chapter 13

Lion down:
Wilson and the king of cats

When I was nearly done Grade 8, I had gone further than any other Maasai I knew. I should have felt settled, but I wanted more. I didn't want to quit school, so I decided to write the national examinations and go to high school, even though I had this niggling voice inside of me saying, "You won't ever go."

I wasn't worried about my marks. I had been, for almost all of my elementary school years, at the top of my class in nearly every subject. Even when I was at home, I would head out with the sheep or the cows, a book in my hand and, as they grazed, I would sit in the shade of an acacia or shepherd's tree and read. By the time I was ten, I could speak and write Maa, Swahili and English fluently.

My favourite stories, however, were still those the elders told by the fire. And some of these stories have actually been written into children's books, like *Kasaine Empira Enye (Kasaine with his Ball)*.

As I grew older, I began to see more and more interest in Maasai culture from foreigners, who would pass by Rotiken's *boma* on their way to see our wildlife. They would stop their jeeps and take our photographs, and when they learned I could speak English, they asked me to recount Maasai stories. I always did, and I came to learn so much from these foreigners—including that the word "safari," which we in Kenya have always used to mean a trip of some sort, to Westerners means coming to Africa to see our lions.

I also came to realize pretty quickly not to tell these foreigners that we Maasai kill lions, or used to kill lions, for these days the Kenyan government only allows us to kill a lion if it is threatening our herds or us. The foreigners loved all of our traditions except for the part about killing lions…and drinking cow's blood. One foreigner, fascinated with our bright clothing, said to me that the Big 5—the "must-sees" for anyone coming on safari—should be changed to the Big 6: elephant, lion, rhinoceros, leopard, buffalo and Maasai.

Not all students in Kenya are eligible for high school. They must have good marks throughout all their years of schooling—but especially in the final year, the equivalent of a North American Grade 8. Students must also do well on a national examination taken near the end of this Grade 8 year.

Students apply to the high schools of their choice before they sit for the national examination. My picks were the Starehe Boys' Centre in Nairobi, one of the top schools in the country, and Moi Secondary School, which was located just a few football fields away from Naikarra Primary School. It too had a great and growing reputation.

I wasn't afraid that my teachers would tell the schools that I was a wayward child. I was the class clown and did, on many occasions, scare the younger students by telling them that if they didn't behave, the pinching man would come and get them. But I was more a jokester than a troublemaker.

My fears were founded on the fact that my father would never support my wanting to go to school for another four years. For one, he never allowed me to do my homework in the *boma*, saying, "You spend too much time in the classroom…now it is time for the cows." If, by candlelight at night, I pulled out one of my textbooks and began reading, he would beat me with a whipping stick. Out on the savannah, in seclusion with the cows, was the only place I could learn and not fear being punished.

But even if I could convince my father to let me attend high school, I would have to deal with the cost. High school tuition in Kenya is about $400 a term, with each year having three terms. I also had to pay for my uniform and the costs for boarding, as all students must live on campus. Simply, I probably wasn't going to be continuing my education.

After I wrote the national examinations, which took two full days to complete, I headed home for the start of the dry season break. Tears welled in the corners of my eyes as I said what I thought was my final goodbye to school.

When I arrived at the *boma*, the women were busy making the local brew for my circumcision, which was scheduled to take place a few days later. I stopped outside the gate and stared at the mamas, bent over the fires stirring the aloe vera liquid. I loved being a Maasai. I never wanted to leave my family or my *boma*. I wanted to care for my cows. But I also wanted to go to school and learn.

And I knew I could contribute more to the Maasai if I did. We were losing our culture. Travel to the Maasai Mara generates much money for Kenya, yet we have the fewest services in terms of teachers, schools, hospital clinics and doctors, and our roads are full of potholes or made out of sand and gravel.

"We need stronger Maasai leaders," Rotiken told me once. "I think that is the only way we can now preserve our culture. We need to send the children to school, but demand that they keep their culture and return home and make us vibrant. Be peaceful, honest leaders and help us progress, not push us backward."

Rotiken has always told me that when future wise men are children, they are quick-witted, and inquisitive.

"As children, the future wise men are always the first to complete tasks among their peers," he had said. These future wise men show an interest in doing things differently, they see the world differently and they become leaders. I felt I was one of these future wise men and I wanted to help my culture thrive by learning all I could at school and then passing my knowledge on to other Maasai.

I was prepared to present my father with these arguments. It was rumoured at this time that Jackson had accomplished the impossible in the cave: slaying the lion in only a month.

I took a deep breath and wiped my eyes. Then I opened the gate.

When I spoke to my *papai*, he was disbelieving at first. "There is no way Letasuna killed the lion from the time the moon appeared full, to the next full moon," my father said, shaking his head. My older brothers, all junior warriors—which is what initiated warriors are called for many years, until they become elders—were shaking their heads as well.

"But *papai*, Jackson is in great physical shape. His mind was clear and he did it. He found a group of eight willing to take him as their ninth and his spear penetrated the lion's skin first."

"A Maasai does not lie," my father said, scratching his chin, "so if he did this and you can do it as well, Enkai willing, then okay, you can go to high school too. But how do you propose paying for these school fees? I cannot sell any of our cows for this! I just will not!"

My heart beat fast. *"Papai,* we can do a *harambee...*you can ask all the Maasai to contribute, like they do during times of drought or when a widow needs help with food." I spat the idea out quickly, perhaps too excitedly, for my father's eyes grew wide.

My father became quiet, very quiet, as my brothers changed the subject to the Maasai elder a few *bomas* from my own who had been caught cheating on his wife with another man's wife. The woman was sent back to her mother, for not being ready to fulfill her duties as a wife, and the elders beat the man. "How shameful," my brothers said, clicking their tongues. "What dishonour!"

That was the end of that conversation. My father didn't mention the *harambee* idea for three full days. Then, as I was emerging from the hot springs after my bath, now wearing a royal blue *shuka* for my circumcision, he stopped me. "I agree," he grunted. "We will do the *harambee* if you succeed in your quest."

"Papai, what made you change your mind?" I asked, stunned.

"Ahh, *olanyor,*" he sighed, which means "my beloved." "I never liked this school thing. I only sent you because Rotiken demanded I do so. But the *oloiboni* said you would be the one to take our stories across the oceans. I must listen to my prophet. And for the last little while, I have been thinking and thinking how best to do that. The answer that came to me from Enkai is that I need to let you go, and let Enkai be your guide. If she wants you to go to school, you will. I have to set you free."

About a week later, I was sitting in front of the *oloiboni* for the second time in my life. This time, I was with the eight other young Maasai, who had been brought together by the elders, with whom I would spend my nights in the cave.

Each of us, or so the elders had thought in making their choices, contributed a talent or gift that the others lacked. The *oloiboni* recognized the gifts I would bring my team: I was brave, a sound leader and a good decision maker. I also had a sense of humour. "Make sure," the *oloiboni* said, as I was getting up to leave, thinking he was done, "that you go in the back. Always go in the back."

When I reached the cave, I focused my mind completely on the tasks I needed to complete, just as I did when I had an examination or essay due at school. Like Terugee, I had spent many of those first few days with my group of nine, finding wood for the fires and learning to slaughter the cows.

We Maasai kill a cow quickly, so it suffers little pain, by hammering a long stick into the back of its head. The cow dies almost instantly and then we turn it over, tie a rope around its feet and lift the bottom part of the cow up to drain its blood out through the tiny incision. We nine collected the blood in calabashes, which we distributed to the others. Then we took great care to cut out the cow's meat, including its ribs, which are the best part for growing warriors to eat to help them grow strong.

The first buffalo I chased got away.

The next day, I decided to go after two dik-diks, very fast and nimble creatures, who took me on a journey through a prickly acacia bush. Breathless and on the verge of collapse, I eventually grabbed one by its hind legs and killed it by piercing its belly with my spear.

The others in the cave, who had been leery of my quest to be ready to head out with a group in search of a lion within one full cycle of the moon, smiled when they saw me return with the dik-dik tossed over my shoulder. "I didn't start chasing dik-diks until recently," one of the veterans in the group said with a laugh, patting me on the back. He'd been in the cave for six months.

A few days after that, I jumped in between two junior warriors having a dispute about how to best encircle a buffalo; there was one grazing near some elephants. One of the young men wanted to race right in and kill it, for it was big and lazy and didn't move much in the midday sun. The other wanted to wait until nightfall, when it moved off.

I remembered Terugee's words about the wind, and relayed to them that the best way to approach a buffalo is from downwind, so it and the elephants will not pick up their smells and charge.

"Why don't you wait until just before the sun sets," I said. "That way the elephants will be tired after their day spent finding food, and the buffalo may be moving off to find some shelter for the night. Approach the creature from downwind," I then repeated. "Always downwind." The two junior warriors returned when the moon was full in the sky. Their faces said it all. Their hunt had been successful and they told everyone it was due to my advice.

As the days passed, I carried boulders up and down the mountain on my back. I also fetched milk from the mamas in the *bomas* at the bottom of the hill. When the moon had waned from full to nearly a sliver, I approached the elder and the most advanced warriors in the cave and pleaded with them: "Please, I am ready. Let me go with the next group. I heard there is a lion nearby."

"No," the junior warriors scoffed. "Many more moons and then you can go and be part of a team. And even then, you will not yet be ready to throw your spear."

The next day, I showed some junior warriors what I could do.

I cradled my spear in the palm of my hand and, using just one finger, lifted it high above my head. It was a great feat, for our spears are very heavy.

Then I threw it, nearly all the way across the clearing.

After that, I raced up the hill with the trunk of a fallen acacia tree in my arms. "See," I said, my eyes pleading. "I am ready. *I am ready!*"

The junior warriors still shook their heads, but the elder stepped forward. He eyed me up and down, his eyes focusing on my burn marks, and then felt the muscles on my arms and legs. "Okay," he eventually said. "You have not spent the time you need in the cave, but your perseverance has convinced me. It is a good Maasai quality to be steadfast. You will go far in life. Try it."

It was easy for me—and the group of eight that I was asked to join—to find the lion pride's tracks in the mud by rivers. According to the tracks, there must have been about six, which included some females, whose paw prints were smaller than the males', and their babies. By the placement of the toes, we could tell the direction they were headed: south toward the Mara River.

Barefooted, we crept after them.

We had set out as the sun was setting over the mountains. Night was falling. We moved swiftly, but quietly, for we were near the forest. The females could pounce at any time, especially since they had babies. They would be extra defensive to protect them.

I pulled up the rear, partly because that was where the *oloiboni* told me to go, and partly because the team of eight, in saying I could join them, had also made it clear that this was just practice for me.

"Some of us have been on hunts six or seven times. It is our turn to spear the lion first," one had said to me.

As we crept further, my heart pounded. My palms started to perspire. I gripped my *conga* as best I could in my left hand and my spear in my right.

Then our group stopped. We heard the breaking of branches in the bushes. Silence followed as we all tried to listen to the breathing of the creature that had made the disturbance. A few squawking *hadada ibis* overhead broke the tension.

I moved my feet away from the riverbank and started slowly walking backwards. The others moved forward, toward where the sound had come from.

Branches broke again, medium-sized branches, too large for a bush baby to break, and an elephant would destroy much more. My eyes scanned the forest, looking for a flash of golden fur.

Then we all heard it.

The cry of a big, wild cat.

I stopped in my tracks when I felt the ground thunder, as it leapt in front of the group. My body was facing the wrong way, but I refused to turn around. I had always been told that the males will boldly come in the front, and the females will slink in through the back. I was waiting for the female.

My peers began to sing and dance, as they had been taught. I started to do the same. That's when a second cat, another male, leapt out from the forest, this time right in front of me. It was close, so close I could feel its hot breath on my knees.

I stopped moving. I became paralyzed as the great big creature, with its lean muscles and pointy sharp teeth, eyed me up and down. Our eyes locked. And indeed, just like Terugee had said, I felt the lion could see right into my soul. I tried to look away, like I was supposed to do. But I couldn't. The lion's eyes had a hypnotic effect on me.

He growled again, his mouth opening so wide I felt my entire arm could slip inside.

I then heard two members of my group come up beside me, and I could see their spears poised, ready to kill.

The lion pawed the ground. I blinked.

I blinked again. Something, a piece of dust, had landed in my eye.

I stepped back from the others, to take it out.

When I looked up, all was quiet.

The lion was dead on the ground, a spear sticking out of its neck.

The other lion had run away.

The nine of us stared at the male lion, and its long golden-white mane. I opened the palm of my hand and saw that what had temporarily blinded me was a piece of red fabric.

"It must have come off your *shuka*," said the warrior standing beside me. He was referring to the plain red *shuka* I was wearing, which my father had given me when I headed to the cave.

I looked at my *shuka*. Indeed, there was now a tear exactly where my spear might have hit if I had thrown it, when I drew it up and then backwards. I gasped

I moved in close. The spear that had drawn a large circle of blood on the animal's clean fur was my own. I had killed the lion.

Chapter 14

Equal measures:
Jackson challenges tradition

Back in Grade 8, before my circumcision, I realized one day I would marry. Sure, part of this knowledge came from starting to be attracted to girls. But I also knew the customs of my tribe. At some point, I would have to wed.

Once a warrior chooses a girlfriend, someone he trusts and loves, that young woman can only speak about the young man positively. By doing so, she is saying she is proud of her warrior boyfriend. The warrior boyfriend must also do the same for her.

Parents are not allowed to know when a Maasai warrior has a girlfriend, because they choose their sons' wives. I knew I would be a lucky Maasai warrior if the girl I chose as my girlfriend was also chosen by my parents to be my wife.

Parents choose their sons and daughters' spouses based on the family's wealth. A Maasai man is considered wealthy if he has a lot of cows. Now, there are some families that have hundreds of cows. That is the family a young man or woman wants to be wed into. To do so, their family must have a good reputation. The warrior brothers must never have flinched or shown pain, or done something shameful, like steal.

Once a mother and father identify a potential bride for their son, they visit the young woman's *boma*. They offer a dowry, usually consisting of three cows, two sheep and blankets for each circumcised male in the family. The dowry also consists of some new *shukas* for the mamas.

If the bride's family approves of the marriage, the mamas will then start making her new bead bracelets and a wedding necklace.

The role of the mamas is to make the young woman as beautiful as she can be, for Maasai women treasure being beautiful. If the bride comes to her wedding day adorned from head to foot in jewelry, including earrings, necklaces, ankle bracelets and rings, she is seen as loved by her family and the groom will look at her adoringly.

On the morning of the wedding, the bride leaves her own *boma* and walks alone to the *boma* of her new family. "You are walking to your new husband," an elder will tell her before she departs. "Follow your husband. Never turn back. If you do, you will be alone, bring shame to both your families and stand as a tree forever and ever."

The first thing the bride does when she reaches her new home is drink milk from a calabash. In doing so, she is said to forget everything about her old life, everything except the final words from the elder. From that day on, she will live with her husband's family. The groom's mama and *papai* are her mama and *papai* now. The groom's generation becomes the bride's generation, too.

Even before my circumcision, my parents were looking for a bride for me. When they attended ceremonies at other *boma*s, my mother would ask questions of the other mamas. "So are there any girls here who could one day marry my son?" she would ask.

Attributes my mother and father looked for were a young woman who would obey me and whose parents were hardworking. My future wife would have to be excellent at beadwork, cooking and cleaning, too. She would ideally be learning how to care for her own future children by caring for her younger siblings.

Usually, Maasai warriors marry after their graduation ceremony, the major event that marks a junior warrior's full entry into adulthood, at which Maasai of the same gernation, from all across the Maasai Mara and the Serengeti, attend.

When I learned that my parents were scouting for my future bride, looking at girls so young they were still playing *boma* in the savannah, I became concerned. Usually, a Maasai warrior marries a woman younger than him. This is true. Before the actual ceremony can take place, of course, she must have gone through puberty and her own circumcision ceremony. Girls can become engaged to warriors when they are children, however, and married as soon as they bleed. It is common for a twelve-year-old girl to be married to a forty-year-old man, usually as his second or third wife.

This was our custom, and I thought nothing of it, to be honest, until my mother and father started proposing names to me of girls they felt were a good fit for me—including one young girl whose adult lower centre teeth hadn't even been pulled yet.

I swallowed hard to hold back my anger. I was still just a boy, daydreaming about football and scoring the winning goal for the district championship, not thinking about settling down on the *boma* and having children of my own.

"Mama," I began slowly, "I just don't know if I want to marry anyone for a long, long time."

My mother put down the necklace she was beading for my sister's circumcision.

"Can I maybe—" I continued, and then stopped, losing the confidence to be honest with my mother.

"Go on," she said quietly.

"Can I maybe," I started and then paused. "Can I maybe choose my own wife?"

My mother stared at me.

"Maybe when I am much older, too," I pressed.

We both fell silent.

I looked down at my feet and listened to the chickens pecking at the bits of grain my mother had scattered for them on the ground outside of her *manyatta*.

I could hear my little sister quietly snoring on the bed of fresh *leleshwa* leaves inside.

"But that is not the way," my mother eventually replied.

"I know, but—"

"Many families want their daughters to be your bride," she continued. "You are one of the bravest warriors for accomplishing that feat with the lion in such little time."

I smiled. "I am honoured," I whispered. "How about this, then. You can find my wife, but wait, don't even look, until I say I am ready. I don't want to get engaged...not for a long time. And I certainly don't want to get engaged to a little girl. Let me finish high school and attend my Maasai graduation and then we can talk about a wife."

My mother nodded. It was her way of saying, "I'll think about it."

I got a slight reprieve, at least. But all our discussions prompted me to start looking around my *boma* and others I visited through the eyes of a future husband. I became very aware, all of a sudden, of the women's downcast eyes, with dark circles underneath. Their slumped shoulders and the lack of joy in their gait saddened me.

Sure, they would perk up when they saw me, or any other Maasai man, looking at them. But this was part of their duty as women. In the same way we Maasai warriors are bred to not show fear, pride or pain, women are taught very early on in their lives to always show their contentment. If they complained about their lives, they risked being beaten by their husbands and bringing shame to their families.

My uncle Rotiken explained to me that Enkai created not just man and cow, but also woman. And she created man and woman to be together. "Maasai believe that the woman was created from the man's rib," he continued. "*Olarasi le kesene*," he whispered in Maa. "A woman was made from man's left side. Her purpose is to be her husband's partner, and he, hers.

"But somehow, long ago, the Maasai came to believe that man is ahead of woman," uncle Rotiken continued. "The legends say it is because women didn't hide their secrets the way men did, and one woman, she told everyone how much property she had. This legend somehow justified men not always having to tell their wives the truth."

"I don't think I like this," I replied. "I also don't believe anyone should be beaten."

"But it is the way."

"Then I do not like our way."

One day shortly after that, I decided to follow the mamas.

I woke when they did. It was still night. The rooster had only called once. I accompanied them as they milked the cows.

After that, they headed out to the savannah to collect firewood. As the sun slowly began to rise, along with the men, the mamas started the fire and began heating the milk. They headed to the nearest river, about twenty minutes away in measured time, to collect water. They made porridge for the children. After everyone had eaten and the dishes were cleaned, the mamas gathered up all the clothes and headed by foot back to the river to do laundry.

After the clothes had been washed, they hung them on the fence and returned to the river with big plastic containers to fill with water.

I became surprisingly tired following the women, for they never stopped to rest.

In the early afternoon, the mamas did their beadwork, sitting on rocks outside their *bomas*, while their babies slept. Then they prepared dinner for the men and boys, who were out walking the sheep, cows and goats.

Our meals were always eaten separately: the males would drink their milk and eat their meat first. The women and girls would eat afterwards, inside the *manyattas*, and it would be usually just leftovers.

As I watched this, I thought of my school and the cafeteria and how the girls and boys would clamour over each other at the tables, touching each other's hands as we shared our food, and laughing and talking as we dipped our *ugali* into gravy.

In my village, however, women were being beaten for transgressions like not having the food ready when their husbands returned from the fields.

I also heard the mamas talking about how school was not important for girls. "She'll be married. What does she need it for?" they would say.

I spoke to their daughters as well. They told me in confidence that they felt they had no choice but to do what they were told.

That July and August, during school break, I had been circumcised and I'd gone to the cave. I knew I had done something truly unbelievable. I'd slain the lion in just a month. But to be truthful, I was thinking of nothing except sitting for the national exams to determine which high school I would attend. Slaying the lion and the festivities that followed were a blur for me. But in the end, I missed only a few weeks of my final term of secondary school. Wilson and my peers started back at the beginning of September, and I joined them about mid-month.

As soon as I saw him, I cornered Wilson.

I told him that I wanted to establish a club for the Maasai girls and boys in school, to encourage discussion of the disparities facing women and girls I had seen in the Mara.

Two Maasai girls were the first to sign up. And every Saturday morning, instead of heading out with the cows, we now returned to school. In the schoolroom we also used for the environmental club, about ten of us talked about women's and girls' issues not just in our *bomas*, but also in all of Kenya and worldwide.

The Maasai girls wanted to speak about female circumcision first.

We had all learned in a health class about female genital cutting and how the West was desperately urging developing countries like Kenya to abolish the practice due to its health risks.

The Maasai don't face HIV/AIDS as extensively as much of sub-Saharan Africa does. Because of practices and beliefs like polygamy and faithfulness, HIV/AIDS of the Maasai can almost always be traced to circumcision and the use of the same unsterilized knife on several individuals.

The girls in our group, along with one of our teachers, came to one of our meetings with research and studies examining the risks to a girl's health from circumcision, including excessive bleeding and complications during childbirth. Armed with this information, we came up with a plan.

Since the mamas in our villages were illiterate and leery of non-Maasai, the best way to raise awareness among them was not through printed campaigns like the Westerners do, but by word of mouth, from other Maasai.

Under the swaying branches of acacia trees, the girls in our club did just that. They convened meetings with the mamas, who beaded as they listened to the girls explain all the risks associated with female circumcision.

Together, they came up with alternatives, like doing the entire circumcision ceremony, which is an important rite of passage for girls entering womanhood, but leaving out the cutting part. The mamas nodded, meaning they would think about it.

Wilson and I began to do the same thing with our *papais*. While boys' circumcision didn't carry the same health risks as girls', we nonetheless encouraged our communities to take boys to health clinics and have doctors do the procedure. We were successful because we explained that the few Maasai men who had died from HIV/AIDS had contracted the virus through dirty knives. But they lived long enough to wed, and to pass the disease on to their wives and babies.

Having HIV/AIDS is taboo among the Maasai. Anyone who has the symptoms—yellowing of the skin, skin lesions, weight loss, sunken eyes and chronic fatigue—is seen as being possessed by an evil spirit. Communities shun such people. Even family members are said to turn their backs on the ill.

In our discussions with the men, Wilson and I, and sometimes Darius, began to share what we had learned at school about the disease and how it is contracted, and ways we could abolish it.

Wilson, Darius and I all agreed the health clinic was where circumcision should be performed, and by a recognized medical doctor. But we weren't sure if anyone would listen. After all, we were young Maasai...and these men were our elders.

It started with our own families. My mother, a midwife and herbalist, agreed to only do circumcision ceremonies from then on if the families stopped short at cutting the girls, and took the boys to the clinic. All the Maasai in my area of the Mara wanted my mother to do their blessings, so they agreed.

This news spread fast around Naikarra, because the Maasai gossip. And soon other Maasai were doing the same. The two girls who first signed up to be part of our club had not been circumcised. They bravely told their mamas that they refused to do so. Their mamas, of course, were furious. But eventually they relented.

We had started a mini-revolution. It was the first time the girls ever stood up to their mamas, and Wilson and I were always there for them when they returned from their *bomas*, their eyes stained from tears, but pleased nonetheless, for they felt they were beginning to be heard.

"It is very empowering to have a voice," Rotiken explained to Wilson and me after we updated him on our activities. "It is both liberating and humbling. A person feels his or her life has meaning. You are doing a good thing. Keep it up."

In our club meetings that followed, Wilson and I began to talk with the girls in the group about the importance of staying in school. "I don't think I want to marry a girl who is uneducated," I said at one point. "I want her to have a mind that can match my own."

Wilson nodded. "And I do not think I want her to be that much younger than me," he added, surprising me, for I had not known that he was thinking the same thing as I was. "What purpose would that serve?" he added. "She would be like a child to me."

"And I only want one wife," Darius said.

The girls went home and told their mamas that the boys wanted to marry girls the same age. And the girls started spreading the word that Maasai warriors across the Mara wanted their wives to be educated, and that they wanted to stop marrying many women. "I want the Maasai woman I marry to be Enkai, with all of her beauty, her wisdom, her grace," Darius said at one point, "not to live as one man with power over another person. This is not the Maasai way."

In our meetings we also discussed the source of this power imbalance. We spoke to Rotiken about it too.

We came up with many answers, but they all led to the same source. We Maasai had not evolved. "We were so scared about losing our culture that we started to lose it nonetheless," Rotiken told us one night when we were all gathered together, "by holding on too tightly to customs and traditions that no longer serve us."

Later, Wilson, Darius and I started a similar club in high school. Eventually, we had about twenty members, more than half of whom were girls who had managed to convince their mothers and fathers that they should go to high school.

In our *bomas* today, particularly around Naikarra, most of the girls are not circumcised and boys go to the health clinic for the procedure. Our campaign was that successful in spreading the word and getting people talking.

Today, we need medical doctors who are Maasai who can perform the procedure. We believe that would really convince all of the elders to change their ways, not just in our communities, but across the Mara and the Serengeti too.

The two girls who originally started the club with us back in Grade 8 left high school to be married. But we were happy, as were they. They were not circumcised. Their marriages took place at age sixteen, not at twelve. And their husbands were just a little bit older than them.

"I am going to make sure," whispered one of the girls, when I bumped into her at the market, "that he only ever takes me as his wife—no seconds or thirds—and that our daughters go to school. And if he ever hits me," she said with a short laugh, "I will take that *conga* of his and hit him back."

Chapter 15

Hazing daze:
Wilson's struggles at high school

When I returned from slaying the lion, I paraded up to my father's *boma* with the lion's mane wrapped around my shoulders and was greeted with shock from my *papai* and his wives, including my mother, and then heavy slaps of congratulations on my back from all my brothers.

My father slaughtered a cow and invited all the elders from far and wide to come for a big feast the next day.

For the ceremony, white chalk lines were drawn on my legs and arms. My face was also painted white. When my mother had made the lion's mane into a headdress, I wore it with honour, even to bed.

For two days straight, it seemed I spent every waking hour leaping up and down with warriors who had come to help me celebrate, including many who had temporarily left their posts in the cave to take part in the ceremony.

We sang many songs and I told everyone what I could about my slaying the lion—not going into too much detail, of course, unless the person was an initiated warrior and had his own experience to share.

"I didn't even know I had killed it," I would always exclaim at the end. "It was like Enkai had taken over my limbs and lifted my arm to perform the action."

When the night of the second day of the festivities became still and the warriors returned to their caves and the elders to their families, my father sat down beside me. As the fire dulled to dying embers, he placed his hand on top of mine and whispered: "I am proud of you." He had never said such words before, for pride is not the way of the Maasai.

We sat silently side by side, watching the rays of the full moon float across the Mara.

My father had sacrificed so much for me, I realized at one point. Mostly, his own pride. He never wanted me to go to school because he was afraid of losing me and of losing face with the Maasai fathers who did not allow their children to go to school. When it became apparent he wouldn't at least physically lose me by letting me attend, he still ran the risk of my leaving both him and the Mara altogether if I continued on the path I was travelling. "If you do become a doctor or a lawyer or a schoolteacher, will you really stay in the Maasai Mara?" my older brother had asked me before I headed to the cave. "I mean, I've been to Nairobi. You can live in a big home with artificial lights that brighten your rooms at night and refrigerators to keep your cow's blood and milk cold."

"Of course I will return to the Mara," I whispered as my father's eyes closed. "I will never leave. The Mara is in my blood."

The *harambee* held in my honour to help me pay for school was one of the most special times in my life. My father told all his wives about it, who told all the mamas in *boma*s across Naikarra, whenever they met at the markets or at the rivers to do laundry. My father also told the elders, who, after their delegation meetings, agreed to take part.

The date was set for the *harambee* ceremony, three days before I was to start high school. The mamas made the local brew and my father chose two goats and a cow to slaughter, for he was expecting more visitors than attended my circumcision and naming ceremonies combined. "You see, we Maasai," he explained, "like helping each other. We like being needed, so everyone will come."

In the meantime, I learned that I had done well on the national exams and had been accepted to Moi Secondary School.

As soon as the sun rose on the day of the *harambee*, I headed to the bushes with my father and some other Maasai warriors to slay the cow and begin the roast. I could feel my breath, slow and deep, steady, as I watched my brothers drain the cow of its blood. I was now one of them. I was a man.

Back at the *boma*, my mother and father were collecting cows, goats and even a few folded, crumpled shilling notes that in some cases had been saved for years in the bottom of tin cans buried under the earth, from the mamas, *papais*, elders and even children who had travelled to our *boma* to help me pay for school.

By the time the *harambee* was done and the donated cows and goats sold, we had raised more than enough money to pay for two years of high school.

Then, the surprise of all surprises came. My father gave me his prized bull. "I will sell it at the market," he said, patting its smooth back as it chewed on some grasses. "He will fetch a lot of money. And that money will be yours."

I'd never cried in front of my father before. Maasai boys just don't do that. But I couldn't contain my emotions. Tears slipped down my cheeks and I hugged my father around the waist, something I had not done since I was a small child. He embraced me too, for a tiny bit. "Go on," he then scolded, wiping his own eyes and shooing me away. "I hope no one saw that!"

The day before I started high school, my mother and I walked to the bus stop and caught the *matatu*, the bouncing minibus that spewed out dark gas fumes and was full of suitcases, cages with clucking chickens and piles of people's groceries. We went to the closest big city, Narok, to buy the items on the list the headmaster of Moi Secondary School had sent me, detailing all the items I needed to live on campus.

My mother and I walked along the aisles of vendors hawking Africana woodcarvings, Maasai drums and knives, and mangoes and papayas, alongside donated and used Western ski jackets and jeans. Oh, and many beads—Maasai beads, or so I thought.

When a short, round Kikuyu man emerged from behind a building and saw me looking at a Maasai wedding necklace, he blushed and quickly grabbed it from my hands.

"What was that all about?" I asked my mother.

She rolled her eyes. "We Maasai have become famous around the world for our bright costumes and beads," she said as we continued walking toward the housewares section of the market. "The tourists snap pictures of us and big stores in cities with cement roads want our beads. Other tribes in Kenya are now making our beads and jewellery and selling them to the tourists. This is one of the reasons why your father and Rotiken want you to go to school. We don't want to lose our culture to others who are making money off of us."

Eventually we made our way to the housewares area. "A mattress," my mother said, passing me a slim foam mattress. "Now blankets."

"But I only want one," I interrupted her, as she picked up two beige cotton throws.

"Why?" my mother asked. "The headmaster says you need two."

"I will deal with the school," I insisted, putting one of the blankets back. "Where I need less, I will take less. I do not need two blankets."

Two pairs of shoes became one pair of shoes. Two plastic plates became one. One fork. One bowl. One cup. We made sure, however, to buy the Bible.

"Is this supposed to be a gift for one of your teachers?" my mother asked, holding the tome up by the edges.

"Yes," I lied, paying for the book and placing it on top of the blanket and my school uniform, which I carried in my arms. The Bible was in Maa, and my mother knew enough Maa words to know what the book was about.

It was the first and only time I ever lied to my mother in my life. I wasn't about to get into explaining that I had to attend Sunday school and church. She and my father had finally embraced my going to high school. I was not so sure they would accept my studying a new religion as well.

On the bus going home, my mama leaned in close and, in a hushed tone, told me some words of advice that I have never forgotten. "Son," she began, "we consider our culture to be highly valuable. And because we do, we value the cultures of others as well. When we don't respect other people's cultures, there is a loss of respect that can drive people to do mean things, like steal and hurt, or even kill.

"If someone passes you and you do not say hello, that person can lose respect for you. They can think bad things of you. Instead of getting angry, however, the Maasai are taught *enkiok mingani*: to put their own anger and hurt in their hearts. Put your ego aside, son, and when you leave Rotiken's home for this place called school, always come from a place of love no matter where you are."

"Go home," said the headmaster, Mr. Makuaki, a short, round man with big, red eyes. I was in my dormitory room. Mr. Makuaki was inspecting the items I brought to make sure I had everything on the list.

"You cannot stay here with what few things you have," he continued. Of course, I had many missing checkmarks on the headmaster's checklist.

I pleaded with the headmaster that I could make do without an extra blanket. I told him about the lion, the cave, how I could run through the forests barefooted, so I surely could play football without cleats. I even said that I was used to eating my food with no utensils, but promised to wash what I had and eat like all the other students with forks and spoons, if I was allowed to stay.

I then told the headmaster how my community had raised as much as they could to send me to high school and how Jackson and I were the only Maasai for many *bomas* that had made it so far in school. "I don't want to waste any of the money that they raised to send me here," I cried. "Please let me stay."

His scowl eventually turned into a grudging smile. "You can stay," he sighed. "I like your determination."

My excitement, however, soon turned to discontent.

"*Mono, Mono, Mono,*" sang some of the older boys as I walked to the shower with my single, small towel. "*Mono, Mono, Mono,*" they sang as they peered over the cement stall to watch me wash myself.

In high school, the years were called Forms. I was in Form 1—and these boys looked to be in the final year of high school, or Form 4.

"Can I have some privacy?" I asked them politely, expecting them to listen.

"*Mono, Mono, Mono,*" they continued, while one picked up my towel, wet the end and then slapped my rear and the backs of my legs with it.

"Stop it! *Stop it!*" I shouted, my face becoming flushed with anger as I tried to grab the towel back from him.

"It is just the start, *Mono, Mono, Mono,*" the boy who had the towel sang as he tossed my towel into the shower, soaking it, and then walked off.

"Mono" means single, and when I returned to my dorm, which I shared with thirty other Form 1 students, I learned that every one of them had been tormented that day too.

One young man from the Kipsigis tribe, who introduced himself with a handshake as Aron Langat, bravely stepped forward, checked to make sure no one was listening on the other side of the doors and proceeded to tell us what his big brother, who had since graduated high school, had told him.

"It is tradition that the older students harass the first-year students," he said, pulling us all into a circle. We wrapped our arms around each other like football players strategizing a play. "He said it will get very bad if we fight back, so brave it. My brother, who is at university now, says in the West they call it hazing. There is nothing we can do."

"How bad can it get?" I asked.

"*Bad*!" he whispered. "Really bad."

The next day the hazing started at morning *chai* break.

When the break was done, about twenty older students emptied their dirty cups on my lap and on the table in front of me. "Your day to clean," they hissed as they left, the staff staring blankly, as if nothing had happened. Scrubbing the cups in the kitchen made me late for geography class.

At lunch, a number of us Form 1s, including Aron, were pushed to the very back of the line, even though our class had been let out earlier than the others. By the time we reached the front, there was little food left and we were given half a portion of *githeri*.

The older students smirked as we walked away with downcast eyes and sat scrunched together at the back of the cafeteria, because there were no tables left for our entire class.

This started happening every day. And I started carrying that one cup of mine everywhere I went. I drank water from sun up to sun down to fill my shrinking stomach, which growled loudly, embarrassing me during quiet time in the library.

On Saturday, which was dorm-cleaning day, I was told by an older student that I had to clean the Form 2 room in addition to my own.

I was hungry, felt faint and wanted to sleep, yet I swept their floors and trotted to the tank of water to wash their sheets.

Just as I was returning with a basket full of clean items to be hung out to dry, a Form 4 student stopped me. "After you do that, go get me some fresh water," he said, his eyes fiery. He handed me a large plastic container with no rope attached to it (that would have helped me balance it on my head). I shook my head, but the boy glared at me.

"Don't tell me you're going to say no," he spat. "If you do, I'll go around and tell everyone what a girl you are." In Kenya only women carry water, so I wasn't worried about my peers thinking I was a girl. They'd think that anyway if they caught me with the container on my head.

I reluctantly took the container, hung my laundry and then fetched some fresh water from the stream, which was about a half-hour walk away from the school.

When I returned, I handed the container to the boy, who turned it upside down and poured it out on my bare feet.

I gasped. "Why did you do that?"

"Go get me some more!" he said, puffing up his chest to show me who was in charge.

I tilted my head to the side and was about to protest when I saw, standing by our dorm door, four more Form 4s, watching our every move. They were flexing their arm muscles. I grumbled and went back to the stream. I returned and had the water poured on my feet again.

When this happened the fifth time, I exploded. "It is because of your wickedness and your weakness that you are doing this to me," I shouted at him. "I didn't fundraise to go to school to fetch water for you. Go and get it for yourself."

As I stormed away to check on the laundry, he kicked up the earth beneath him and gestured for his friends. But they didn't come after me.

By evening, it had been circulated around the school that a Form 1 student had stood up to one of the older boys. The rumour further abounded that the Form 1 student was on drugs, including cocaine and marijuana. "He'll be kicked out of school, for sure," one of my Form 1 peers said as we turned off the lights, not knowing that the rumours were about me. "The headmaster is going to search all of the Form 1 belongings in the morning to discover the culprit."

My mind churned. "Are these older boys going to hide these drugs in my bags so I get kicked out?" I thought to myself.

I had a restless sleep, worrying the entire night about my fate. I finally fell asleep just as the rooster called for the first time. I awoke on his second song. I leapt up and into my school uniform and black oxford shoes, even though it was Sunday. I headed straight to the headmaster's house and knocked on his door.

He answered, rubbing first his tired eyes and then his messy hair. He was wearing a black-and-white striped dressing gown.

"What is it, son?" he asked, looking up into the sky. "It's not even sunrise yet."

"Look," I began, my knees shaking. "I am the boy who stood up to the Form 4 student yesterday." I told the headmaster what the boy had made me do, and what I had said to him on the fifth time he had poured the water on my feet. "He and his friends are now spreading rumours all around the school that I use drugs. Look," I said, fighting back tears. "I am not from the city. I know about these drugs only from my social studies class in elementary school. On the Mara we only have cow's blood, milk and medicines."

"Don't worry, lad," the headmaster said, patting me on the shoulder. "I believe you."

He shut his door and returned to sleep.

While I wasn't blackmailed or kicked out of school, the abuse didn't stop.

The cooks now made me get my food last of everyone, including all the Form 1s. The older students tripped me on the football field during games. And I spent my Saturdays cleaning other boys' underwear.

At night time, the other Form 1 students and I talked in hushed tones, about what we were going through. "One day, I will be president of Kenya," said Aron, his fist in the air, his face perspiring and flushed from having spent the day cleaning toilets. "Then I'll get back at these kids who do this to us!"

As the others cheered, I started to say no, quietly and then more loudly. "No!"

That's when I told Aron and my friends in Form 1 what my mother had said on her way back from shopping.

"We consider our culture to be highly valuable. And because we do, we value the cultures of others as well. *Enkiok mingani*," I repeated several times. "This means to put your anger and hurt inside your heart."

A few weeks later, just before the end of my first year of high school, two of my teachers approached me. They sat me down in a vacant classroom and said that I had top marks in all my subjects and that I was a positive influence on the other students in Form 1. "Will you be the dormitory representative next year, for all the Form 1s and 2s?" asked the headmaster, Mr. Makuaki.

"Yes," I said, sitting up straight. "Of course! But I want to stop this horrible practice that Aron says is called hazing. I want the Form 1s to feel they are here for school, not to be the servants of the Form 3s and Form 4s. Most of all, I want to get the teachers and the staff, including the cooks—who either turn a blind eye or worse, do what the Form 4s tell them—to stop! I want there to be consequences to any form of violence against younger students."

The teachers nodded, and explained that I would be able to be on a committee of teachers and older students. I could address all of these concerns there.

When dawn broke a few mornings later, I shivered, as I remembered something that I had forgotten. A Maasai prophecy of long ago said that violence would come, violence that would escalate from homes to school-yards to villages and then even the country.

As I started to pack my things for holidays, I told myself that I would have to move fast, starting with talking to the cooks about the food portions and explaining that the Form 1s were starved. They had to feed them their full portions.

Then I would move on to the football coaches and teachers who ignored the actions of the older students.

Somehow, in some way, I would relay to the Form 4s how their actions against the first-year students really hurt us and hindered our learning. Not to mention our expectations that school is supposed to be a place of equality and nurturing.

Our school, which had many of the tribes of our great nation represented within our dormitories and classrooms, was just a mini version of all of Kenya. If we could put in place a peaceful, non-violent environment, all of us students would go out into the world living by these principles, and show others how to do so, as well. I was sure of it.

Chapter 16

Club life: Jackson and the emergence of the Maasai

The hazing got to me too, as I endured all that Wilson did. I was so proud of him for standing up to the Form 4s. He unfortunately ended up taking on the brunt of the abuse for all of us for a while because of his defiance, until he got the teachers, cooks, students and headmaster to listen to him. In Form 2 all the hazing stopped by midwinter.

With that, Wilson and I were finally free to focus our minds on more positive endeavours, like starting an environment club, similar to the one we had established in elementary school.

We Maasai grew up being part of Kenya's wildlife. I lived side-by-side with the elegant elephants, the bashful baboons, the insane wildebeest and the naughty hyenas. But I found many of the non-Maasai students, especially those from cities, didn't know much about this country we call home. Some had never seen lions, let alone elephants, giraffes, wildebeest or antelopes.

Wilson and I were also inspired by our president Daniel Moi to start the club. In our politics class, we learned that in 1989, he burned twelve tonnes of seized elephant ivory, which was and still is illegal to take. Nonetheless, elephant ivory is a sought-after commodity for collectors and for the makers of Chinese herbal medicines. When President Moi burned the ivory, an estimated $10 million went up in smoke. But he didn't care. He did it to show the world that Kenyans came first. That he would end the vicious slaughter and abuse of our wildlife.

The Maasai knew all too well the horrors of the ivory trade, having seen elephants and their facial wounds after the ivory was removed—and in some cases, their dead carcasses. Sadly, the practice of ivory trafficking just went further underground.

And despite bans on the poaching of other wildlife, like rhinoceros, we Maasai all saw that the trade continued, illegally.

The Maasai were also witnessing deforestation and the effects of global warming. Due to the lumber trade, foreign companies were coming to our land and taking our trees for paper and wooden products. And drought was now so frequent that we had to change our diet, just in the span of my childhood.

Wilson and I started our environment club with a hope to learn as much as we could about global warming, drought and poaching. We also started the club to share our knowledge and experiences as Maasai with those who didn't grow up chasing dik-diks through bushes.

Wilson and I began by describing to other students how all of Enkai's creations, which included the trees, animals and humans, live in harmony, and how when something comes in and pushes just one part of that harmony out of balance, it impacts the whole.

The teachers we invited spoke about carbon emissions and how the world is heating up, and how this heat is most felt along the equator, which Kenya crosses. "So whereas people in perhaps the United States may not be experiencing the impact of global warming first hand," one instructor explained, "those people living in countries in the earth's middle—many of which are still developing—are going through weather disruptions like droughts." The droughts, he explained, bring on famines that force people to move in search of water and food. "In some places, like the Sudan and Somalia, the migrating people walk right into warring tribes and groups," he continued. "The biggest producers of carbon emissions are businesses in countries who do not realize what they are doing to the rest of the world."

Once a week, our entire environment club headed out to the lush parts of our forest and sought out small trees. We dug up the trees and replanted them in barren areas, including around the school. We even invited a woman named Wangari Maathai to give a lecture. She started a movement in Kenya to replenish the land by encouraging women to plant trees.With the income these women earned planting the trees, they bought cash crops that they planted in the fertile earth beneath the trees. The crop yields were used to feed their children more balanced and nutritious meals. And they sold anything left over at the markets.

Sadly, Wangari could not come because of a busy schedule, having recently won the Nobel Peace Prize for her work.

In the club, I began to slowly see my place in the cycle of nature. Not among the wildlife, for I had always seen that, but within a larger whole, and with a purpose inside of me that I had not recognized before. The non-Maasai in our group were eager to learn my Maasai ways. I never thought it would be like that. I thought going to school meant I would learn Western things, not the other way round.

The attention got me thinking: how could Enkai create our beautiful mountains and seas, most of which I had only seen in textbooks, and then create the capacity for us to destroy it all? I just couldn't understand.

I fell into a deep funk that lasted a long time. I was so fearful that everything good could be taken away. Like any darkness, however, there was light there. From the shadows of my mind emerged important questions I began asking myself about my life.

"How can I make a difference? What is my purpose? What is my role in making sure the good remains good?"

Like many African boys, one dream I did harbour was to become a professional footballer. During the time I was stuck in that melancholy, only two things could lift me up. The first was that field of shorn grasses, over which I would run, as fast as I could, zigzagging my way down to shoot a goal. *Whoosh*...I can still hear the ball whizzing through the air after a kick that came with the spirit and strength of an elephant.

Also like most Africans, my first football was made of plastic bags, wrapped together and tied with elastics.

On the savannah, near my *boma*, I made two goals out of mud, stones and twigs. I couldn't find any wire or mesh to complete the goals, so the ball often went bouncing across the field, with us laughing as we chased after it.

Of course we didn't have television in our *bomas*, so I learned all my moves at school. I then taught these moves to the Maasai children not attending school (and to the adults, who also wanted to learn).

Maasai elders have never played football, or any sport for that matter, other than running, our leaping games and carrying boulders on their shoulders to prepare for slaying the lion.

As a result, their hand-eye coordination wasn't so great. Some of the Maasai men had such long legs that they fell flat on their faces when they tried to dribble the ball down the field. Others fell backwards when they went to kick the ball and missed. And some just gave up and sat on the sidelines watching us kids, who were more natural at picking up new activities.

Two men, however, refused to give up after their failed attempts to kick the ball. These men collided with each other at one point, both breaking bones in their legs, which our mamas wrapped in heated cow dung to help heal.

I was one of the youngest students to ever make it onto the high school team, which I did in Form 1. Over the four years of high school, I moved my way up from playing defense to striker. While I never grew very tall, like some Maasai, I made up for it with speed.

I was good at not just football but also volleyball, and in Form 2 I was asked to be co-captain of all the sports teams. My duties included coordinating the girls' field hockey games and helping the football and volleyball teams select their players. I was elected to this position for Forms 3 and 4, too, which was a great honour.

In Form 4, I also joined the dance team. At the tryouts, the Kipsigis did their tribal dances. The Kikuyus did theirs. There were so many Maasai who signed up that the instructor decided we would form a separate team and perform traditional Maasai dances in the competitions.

The males, including me, performed two numbers, one in which we did *adumu*, our jumping dance, and another in which we all played the antelope horn.

The Maasai make an instrument from the horns of dead antelopes they find on the Mara. We clean the horn and then poke holes in it. When a warrior blows into one end of the horn and runs his fingers over the holes, it makes beautiful music, like that from a flute, or the sound of our mothers' singing drifting in the wind over the Mara.

Our Maasai team won the district championships. We then came third at the provisional games, enabling us to go to the finals in Nairobi.

By the time I was in Form 4, I had seen many cars and buses kicking up dust and sand on the roads of the Maasai Mara. I had taken *matatus*. I was no longer afraid, like I was when I was small, that the vehicles were animals that swallowed Maasai children, clothes and all.

But I had never been to Nairobi. I had never set foot in a big city, only the markets of Narok.

While the bus taking us to Nairobi bumped along the dusty, potholed streets of southern Kenya, I rehearsed in my head my roles in our performances. In addition to playing the antelope horn, which I had mastered in the cave, and the *adumu*, our dance teacher had decided to add a third number for our performance in Nairobi. The *Antipoti* is the song for men, in which we sing back and forth to each other, much like we do when we visit the *oloiboni*. In this performance, I was to roar like a lion.

After that, the Maasai girls on the team were to sing the *Olesikanpa*, a lullaby, while rocking pretend babies in their arms to sleep. These young women, most of whom were part of our club, had the sweetest, highest voices I had ever heard. I knew they were going to wow the audience. But I wasn't so sure about me!

My thoughts turned from doubts about my performance to my surroundings as the bus made its way into the Great Rift Valley of rolling hills and then up a tall embankment. I looked down, out the dusty window, and saw Agoolonana's line, which was visible as a clearing in between the trees and bald patches on the brown, dry grasses.

My pulse quickened as we then made our way into the suburbs of Nairobi and the beiges and golden hues of the Great Rift Valley were replaced with the reds of the tall cement buildings. More and more buses, *matatus* and cars joined us on the roads, along with big trucks that slowed as they chugged their way up the hills.

Then all I could hear, even above the chattering of my peers, was the honking of horns.

I covered my ears and closed my eyes, until the bus stopped in what our headmaster said was downtown. As I stepped off the bus, I looked over at a park full of people, with a bronze statue of Mzee Jomo Kenyatta, Kenya's first president, in the middle.

I then stared into the sky, which was partially blocked by buildings far taller than any tree or giraffe I had seen, and full of glass. I shielded my face in my hands. My body began to tremble, and for a moment my breathing became choked.

I had, of course, heard of skyscrapers before, but it was a lot different seeing them with my own eyes.

I turned to the headmaster, who had come up beside me. "Sir," I whispered, not wanting the other Maasai, many of whom had been to the city before, to see my fear. "Will these not fall? Will not the glass come crashing down and slice me in two?"

His big hearty laugh shook his large round belly, so much so that I thought he would pop the buttons on his shirt. "No," he replied. "In between the glass, these buildings are made of cement. They will stand tall, like you."

I didn't fully believe him, but as we walked the streets full of people, the skyscrapers didn't come crashing down...so I felt a little safer.

I didn't eat for the entire twenty-four hours we were in Nairobi, as I was too afraid to try the "french fries" the hotel gave us, which looked like skinny fingers to me. The only other option was chicken. But my mother had told me that chicken bones are too tiny and could get stuck in my throat—Maasai don't eat chicken. So I survived on milk and prayed to Enkai that I had enough energy to get me through everything.

When we arrived at the auditorium where we were to perform, I heard, in whispered conversations among the other competitors, that President Daniel Moi was in the stands.

I wasn't nervous when our headmaster confirmed that the rumours were true. I was curious, so curious that when we took to the stage and the spotlights came on, I lifted one of my hands to shield my eyes from the light and scanned the seats.

I paid no attention to the music or my team. I wanted to see the president, the man who my school was named after and who was brave enough to burn twelve tonnes of ivory.

As a result, I jumped up during the performance, when everyone else went down. I turned to the left, when everyone turned to the right. I stopped mid-routine and shook my head, criticizing myself right in the middle of the number by slapping my forehead. "Performing well is far more important than seeing this president. If you are meant to meet him, you will," I told myself.

I performed flawlessly for the rest of the number and the two that followed.

When we were done, everyone in the troupe, including me, had a good laugh at my mistakes. I was embarrassed and apologized. We were happy nonetheless, for the school, at least in the time I had been there, had never come so far in the competition. We didn't care if we came in last.

When all the groups were finished performing, the master of ceremonies took the stage and introduced President Moi.

I stretched my neck to peer over the crowd of students who had gathered backstage to look at him. All I could see was just a tiny bit of the back of his head.

"Moi Secondary School!" the announcer then said, in a booming voice that echoed through the jam-packed auditorium.

Everyone started to clap and cheer, except my group, some of whom were scratching their heads, while others looked around to see what was going on.

A tall boy from one of the Nairobi schools pushed me out toward the stage. I stopped and turned, thinking it was a joke. Then I saw our head-master waving for all of us to follow him. We pushed our way through the crowd of competitors standing in the wings and took centre stage.

We had come first!

I found myself shaking the hand of our president, after he had given one of my teammates the trophy.

I was stunned, and remained so until the headmaster cupped his hands and whispered in my ear that the judges thought my moves were part of the routine. As we made our way to the bus, I was standing tall. I could breathe normally again, now that the performance was finished, and I was finally convinced that those tall buildings that reflected the colours of the sky wouldn't fall on me.

On the bus ride home, I thought back to the life question. You see, I still couldn't understand why Enkai would create such beauty in the form of our people, our women, our environment, only to have her very same creations turn against and destroy each other. Rotiken told me once that I might well spend my entire life searching for the answer.

But the *oloiboni* told Darius that he would be a great leader of his people. The prophet told Wilson that he would take the Maasai to the West. And he told me that I would be great support for both of them.

When I looked into President Daniel Moi's eyes I saw compassion and understanding, but after, I also remembered all of the corruption that Kenyans have suffered under his rule, including his suppression of any form of freedom of speech, and the money that it is alleged he and his ministers stole from the public. He had lost something since he boldly burned the ivory and declared to the world, "We are taking back our wild-life and protecting it!"

There was a darkness covering his heart like a cloak, the way one did my own when I fell into my funk. After I looked into his eyes, I said to myself: "If I ever go into politics, I will never lose the soul of the Maasai, which is about preserving our land, giving and receiving, and making sure everyone is cared for."

"That's it!" I declared out loud as our bus made its way down the steep hill into the Great Rift Valley, beginning our return trip to our school at the far corner of the Maasai Mara. My eyes landed once again on Agoolonana's line. "I will go into politics," I said out loud. "That is my purpose in life. I will be the Maasai leader that brings justice and fairness back to my people, and brings the Maasai values of justice and fairness to other Kenyans."

Chapter 17

Power of the protest:
Wilson leads with peace

Jackson was fortunate. When he and the dance troupe made it all the way to the national championships in Nairobi, our school finally had a bus. He didn't have to worry about how he was going to get to the city.

But getting that bus was not an easy task, When Jackson's group won, we all celebrated, not just for their victory on stage, but for our victory as a school.

Let me backtrack a bit.

At the start of Form 3, we didn't have a bus. Students often had to walk twenty kilometres, sometimes more, to attend sports events and music and dance recitals at the nearest school. For events at other schools the students would split up into groups and grab public buses or *matatus,* or hitchhike for rides in vans and trucks or on the backs of motorbikes.

For years, our school leaders had been promising the students that they would purchase a bus. All of the high schools we competed against had their own buses, and in some cases more than one. The promises from our headmaster and other school officials started when I was in Form 1. "We *will* buy you your bus." But by Form 3, we were still without one and the students were getting upset.

One day, near the end of the term, the student captain threatened that if the school didn't buy a bus right then and there, the students would stage a protest and go on strike.

"The bus is coming! The bus is coming!" a school administrator announced during a meeting, his face red. He was full of fear, I knew, because student protests in Kenya often escalated into violence. In some schools, students had set classrooms ablaze.

Recently, the high school in Narok had had several of its dormitories destroyed by student protesters. A teacher was even beaten and had to spend time in the hospital. In a Nairobi school uprising, a student had entered his class with a gun.

After these and other incidents, Kenya's national newspaper headlines screamed: *The Country's Students are Out of Control.*

This may seem like nothing to a Western school-aged child. But in many developing countries revolutions have taken place, with the impetus for change often starting among students.

Despite the school administrator's promise, Moi Secondary School still didn't buy the bus. And the students laid their plans. They were walking out...they were going on strike!

On the eve of the strike, I had to say something. I saw nothing good coming our way. As I paced the hallway of my dorm, my mind churned with the prophecy Rotiken had told me: "Long ago, the wise men predicted there would be a time in Kenya's history of great bloodshed. Tribes would turn on other tribes..."

As my body shivered, I asked myself, "Is this the start?"

Eventually, I couldn't contain my concerns that violence would escalate, so I left the dormitory determined to do something.

A large crowd of students had gathered in the courtyard. The older boys, particularly those in Form 4, were enraged, jostling their fists up in the air and screaming, "Down with the school! Down with the school!"

Darius came up beside me. Jackson moved to my other side. "We need to stop this," Darius leaned over and said. "Someone is going to get hurt."

"But how can we get them to listen?" I exclaimed, scanning the crowd of angry students, many with reddened eyes and puffed-up chests.

"Not 'we,'" Jackson replied, turning to look me in the eyes. "You! Darius may be a leader within our community. But non-Maasai don't follow our customs. They won't listen to him."

I looked at Darius, who nodded.

"As for me, well, I am popular in sports, but not politics, at least not yet. You, however, have been speaking out on issues since Form 1. The students listen to you."

"What do I say?" I asked.

"I will go first, because the rowdy boys, all those who are throwing around the most power and inciting the others, play football. They will respect me if I ask them to stop their chanting and listen. Then you can speak to the entire school after that."

There was nothing else we could do, so I mouthed the word "yes." Jackson stood up on a *chair*, smoothed down his pants and cleared his throat.

I could see his forehead perspiring as he started banging on a Maasai drum made of cow skin. When the crowd was still, Jackson declared in a big booming voice: "Before you do anything, before you leave this field, I want you to listen to Wilson."

Some of the football team members booed.

"Do you not trust me?" Jackson said directly to them.

Their voices quieted. "When I first came to school, I did so to learn," Jackson said, as the students slowly turned their full attention to him. "I wanted to learn reading and writing, math and science. I have loved every minute of it. But what has also become clear to me, to Darius, to Wilson," he said, waving his hand to both us, "is that you, too, want to learn about we Maasai and our traditions."

"Not now," someone from the crowd shouted.

"Yes, now," Jackson replied. "There is a way we can all work together," he continued, ignoring the jeers from the football players. "A way in which the best of Western culture and the best of Maasai culture can walk hand in hand."

"Not now, Jackson," one of the Form 4 boys yelled.

"Yes, now," Jackson replied in a confident voice, belying the nervousness I could see in his shaking hands. "We all know what could happen here today if we allow this protest to get out of hand. I want you to listen to Wilson, just give him a chance."

As Jackson talked, Darius pulled me aside. "I understand your fears. Most of the students are from cities, not from the Mara, and they don't have respect for our ways. But you have to speak to them, to somehow make them listen, so we can avoid any violence."

After Jackson had won the crowd's attention, he turned the platform over to me.

"Hello everyone," I said, in a shaky voice.

"I know you are all very angry. We have wanted a school bus for a very long time and our complaints have fallen on ears that do not hear us. But destroying the school, vandalism—or worse, hurting teachers—will not solve anything. What future will you have if you have no school to attend? What future will you have if you throw a stone and get kicked out of school, never able to return?

"In our Maasai *bomas*, we are very sad that we have to travel now almost every year to Tanzania with our cows to escape the droughts. But we do not burn down or hurt our *bomas* or our cows to show our anger at the Kenyan government for not telling the world about our problems and doing something about them.

"It is the same with this school. It is yours. It is where you learn, where you become smart. If you destroy it, you destroy something that belongs to you...you destroy your future. The administration will have won, for all of you will be kicked out and they won't need to buy a bus because there won't be any students left!

"All we can do is ask again the elders of this school, the headmaster and the senior teachers, to meet. Walk away from your classes until they agree to this meeting and buy us a bus. But do not cast any stone. It is not your place to do so."

I sat down, out of breath, my knees shaking.

The crowd remained quiet.

I breathed slowly and steadily, hoping that the silence meant they were thinking seriously about what I had said. I could even hear Jackson and Darius' hearts beating. We were all afraid, wondering which direction the students would choose.

Suddenly, a Kikuyu student leapt up on the vacant *chair* beside Jackson. He thrust his fist in the air, the way he had before. But instead of inciting violence, he got the crowd to agree to what I had said.

"Tomorrow morning, walk out of the compound, quietly and peacefully. Don't look back. And don't touch anything on the way out. Wilson is right. If we hurt this school or its teachers, all our learning and studying will go down the drain."

The next day, all of us did walk out—but peacefully. We Maasai students who lived nearby planned to return to our villages, while the other students would take *matatus* into Narok and then buses into Nairobi or wherever they lived.

Those of us heading home walked for several miles together, until some of the students stopped and said they were hungry. Their hunger prompted them to start inciting the crowd, which numbered about three hundred, to attack the markets in Narok and steal food.

Jackson intervened again. He stood up on a rock and faced everyone. He told them to quiet down. He then gestured for me to take over.

Darius patted me on the back for encouragement as I leapt up on the rock Jackson had been on. I told the crowd to shush.

"You should be very proud," I began, "that we left the school with no vandalism or violence. To resort to violence now, by stealing food, would only weaken our case. Right now the school officials are probably thinking very hard about giving in to our demands for a bus because of how peacefully we left the school. If we create trouble now, all our good efforts will be lost. I know you are hungry. So am I. But we need to forge ahead with pride, not spiral down into madness to satisfying our basic needs."

Darius suggested that I invite everyone to the Maasai villages to drink some milk and have some porridge.

I agreed, hoping Rotiken's wives would not be too angry at my arriving with so many students. Darius helped out by taking a third of the group to his village, while Jackson took another third to Jonathon's *boma*.

About a month into our strike, all the students safely back with their families, the radio announced that Moi Secondary School had bought us our school bus.

We won!

The radio also said that the students on strike could return to school. But we had to arrive, the announcer reported, with our parents.

We crowded onto the football field and one by one, with our mothers and fathers, attended meetings inside the school with school officials. Some students emerged from these meetings with their eyes puffy from crying, saying they had been sent home, suspended, or in some cases expelled. The school officials had told the students' parents that they needed discipline. The rest of us assumed it was because they were part of the strike. The teachers, we were told, knew information about the strike that they could only have received from other students. This shocked us all. I thought I was about to be expelled for sure.

All twenty of the high school's teachers were present, along with the headmaster, when my mother and I crept into the staff room where the meetings were taking place. They sat in a semicircle in the small room. The windows were closed and the air was thick with dust and heat.

My mother sat down facing the teachers, with me beside her. My father was out tending the cows and couldn't come, she had me explain to the teachers, none of whom could speak Maa.

She then nodded hello to everyone.

"You must be very proud of your son," the headmaster began. My back stiffened and my eyes popped open. I was expecting to hear: "Your son needs to pack his bags and leave school immediately."

My mother smiled weakly when I translated.

"He should be commended," said one of the teachers.

"Why?" I asked.

"Because, from what we have heard from other students, you stopped your peers from resorting to violence," said the headmaster.

"That took great courage," added Ole Mateu, my chemistry teacher. "You showed real Maasai leadership."

"What about all the students who left here crying and being expelled?" I asked.

"They were trying to incite riots," replied the headmaster. "We want them to think about some things before they return to school. They weren't expelled," he explained. "They were suspended."

As my mother and I stood up to leave, the headmaster cleared his throat and asked me to stay for a minute. He and the teachers crowded around each other, whispering in hushed tones, before facing my mother and me. "We want you to be student captain of the school next year," the headmaster said. "Wilson, will you agree?"

That night, I sat with Darius and Jackson near the football field, underneath the acacia nilotica trees Jackson and I had planted with the environment club. They were commended during their meetings as well. We were talking about the events of the past few days.

"How can I lead my school?" I asked at one point. "How can I be student captain?"

"Don't think about it," replied Darius. "Let Enkai lead through you, like she did during the strike."

"The reason you were chosen," Jackson added, "is because you have already shown great leadership. You have already shown you are a role model. In fact, I'd say you have shown you are a leader since the day you set foot in this school."

"So just keep being you," Darius said with a smile. "Keep being a Maasai, in a Western school."

"School," I told the assembly in my first formal speech as student captain at the start of Form 4, "is like a river. Students come and go, like water flows from one river to the next and eventually out to the sea. For these four years you are in high school, it is like being on the Mara River, being guided out to the sea of life. It is important that we all make our boat, the high school, as strong as possible, so we can navigate the great rapids—and the stillness that follows—to get to our destinations the best we can.

"Students, all students, are on this boat together," I continued. "We are one and we float down this river as one. We need to remember that whenever we feel tempted to single someone out. To disrupt one person's education is to disrupt the entire school. To support one student, is to support us all."

As I left the stage, I said a silent prayer: "Work through me and let me be the leader you want me to be."

Chapter 18

A *future fulfilled:* Jackson and friends learn their fate

Not long after my school troupe won the national dance championship, Darius, Wilson and I began debating whether or not to take a year off high school to attend our Maasai generation's graduation ceremony. It was a difficult decision. Wilson and I wanted to finish Form 4 and graduate high school. Going to the Maasai graduation, which usually takes a full year, would mean missing out on that.

Darius, who was in Form 3 because he had taken a year off school to be in the cave, didn't want to fall further behind.

We were all torn as to what to do.

The Maasai graduation ceremony happens only once every fifteen years or so. I say "or so" because the ceremonies happen on Maasai time, which means whenever the elders say the generation is complete and all those who needed to be initiated have been initiated.

Our parents prepare their entire lives for their sons' graduations. Our mamas and *papais* save the best cows. Our mamas set aside the thickest and brightest blankets.

The graduation ceremony typically starts, I had been told, with those who will be graduating, along with their mamas and *papais* (the younger siblings stay home with the other mamas or their aunties) heading on foot across the Mara, to the savannah not far from the *boma* belonging to Oloruma, the prophet. In the middle of the grasses, they create new temporary *boma*s, in which they live for a full twelve months among the other Maasai warriors of our age set and their parents, who have travelled from all the corners of Maasailand.

"You know I want to be a teacher one day," Darius said, in his soft yet authoritative voice. "I want to teach Maasai children in Kenya's schools.

But I don't see any money yet for teachers college. I will have to sell some cows and maybe work at a game reserve for a few years after high school. And one day, for sure, I will go to university. But I will never have another Maasai graduation."

What was unsaid between us was the prediction that Darius would be a Maasai leader. Darius had taken his words very seriously. Over the years, he had spent all his spare time with Maasai elders and his peers, listening to their dreams and hopes for the future, their worries and their pains.

Darius silently stood up and walked the savannah alone, thinking about what he should do. As Wilson and I watched him become a black speck against the setting sun, we could hear hyenas baying in the distance.

Darius returned several hours later, when we had just finished our math homework. "I'm going to go," he said. "I'm leaving school for the graduation."

Wilson and I had decided we would remain. The decision came easily, for we knew that Darius would represent us, and we also knew our parents would accept our choice.

Darius wrote to us every month, detailing all of his experiences, starting with when he arrived back at his *boma*. He said he became apprehensive, with a lump forming in his throat, the moment he entered his mother's *manyatta* and began helping her pack.

Darius' mother had already packed up some food, including rice and beans she had bought at the market, and had wrapped everything in blankets. Darius' *papai* had told him that two donkeys would carry all their possessions for their year-long stay at the ceremony site, and they would bring along five cows and ten goats to be slaughtered.

All the while, Darius wrote, he felt a stirring within him that he could not explain. He wanted to believe he was just excited about the actual graduation. He hadn't realized, until arriving home, how much attending the graduation ceremony actually meant to him.

That first night back at home, he prepared a bed of cow skins and blankets on the ground near the cows' *boma*. For a long time, he lay awake staring at the stars and the Milky Way, which was bright and beckoned him to his dreams. His eyelids fluttered when the moon was above him, and then flashed open when he saw a falling star. He didn't sleep at all after that.

The next day opened with a mist that covered the ground and dampened Darius' face and head. But the sun soon kissed the dampness dry.

Shortly after a breakfast of cow's blood and milk, Darius and his mama and *papai* said goodbye to the rest of the family and began their silent walk across the Mara.

As he left, Darius waved goodbye to his older brothers, who had promised to join him for the final days of the festivities. Despite all the stories they had told him about their graduation, Darius somehow felt as he looked toward the east, toward the graduation ceremony, that his experience would be different. "I just have a feeling," he wrote to me, "that my life is about to change forever."

As soon as Darius arrived at the field near the *oloiboni's boma*, he headed out to the woods with a few other young warriors to collect wood. They cut down the branches of white bush, orange croton and acacia trees, to be used for the fences. Then they gathered smaller branches and twigs to use for firewood.

Their mothers, meanwhile, were collecting mud, rocks and cow dung to build the walls of the *manyattas*, while the young warriors' *papais* had started to dig the foundations.

There were about four hundred junior warriors, plus their parents, in the one giant, newly built *boma* where Darius ended up living. All of the inhabitants worked together for two full moon cycles to build their *manyattas*, *boma*s for the cows and a fence that spanned the length of two big football pitches to protect everyone from the lions.

All the while the junior warriors sang songs about things like finding their wives, slaying the lion and the pinching man, and what he did to them when they were children.

At night, the junior warriors huddled together and recounted their experiences of slaying the lion, which they could do now that they were all initiated warriors. Each story was as exciting and suspenseful as the last.

Darius recounted not only slaying the lion as part of his initiation, but how he went on to kill another four lions: two that had been trying to attack his *boma*, and another two that had attempted to get his cows when he was travelling to Tanzania to escape the drought.

Darius learned that all the warriors had killed more lions than just the one during their initiation—all, of course, in order to protect their cows.

And as was tradition, the warriors' mamas all pinned the manes of all the lions that their graduating sons had killed to the walls of their makeshift *manyattas* at the graduation *boma*. When they returned to their permanent *bomas*, these manes would be displayed on the walls of their *manyattas*. If a mama was fortunate to have many sons, all the walls of her home could be covered in lion manes.

"We want you to go and get the root of *oseki*," a group of elders told Darius a few months into the graduation, the root of a sandpaper tree. Darius lifted his fingers to scratch his chin, but then thought otherwise. He knew the action might show confusion, and the elders could look unfavourably upon him and his family if he did. Darius just nodded and set off on his own.

Since the junior warriors had finished helping build the mamas' *manyattas* and constructing the fence, the elders had been giving assignments to all of them as part of their graduation duties. Most of the other junior warriors, Darius noted, were being given easy things to do, like fetch *leleshwa* leaves for one of the mamas' beds or milk from a nearby village.

Darius, on the other hand, was being asked the impossible. He thought of speaking to his father about it that night when he returned from his journey, hoping that he would successfully find the root. If he wasn't, he'd have to stay out until he did.

Darius went deep into the bush, nearing a forest that he did not plan on entering. His nails became blackened from digging around in the earth, looking for this root. Luckily, he found what he was looking for just as the sun began to set and scurried back to the *boma* before night fell.

After he handed over the root of the sandpaper tree to the elders, he returned to his mother's *manyatta*. But before he could ask his father for a talk, two elders and his father whisked him away to meet with two other men at the far end of the *boma*.

"The men we are about to meet," his *papai* explained as they walked, "have been bickering over whose cow to slaughter for the main ceremony at the beginning of the graduation. Both want their cows to be first."

When they arrived, the men were red-faced and excited. They spoke quickly and at the same time, with their hands waving in the air in animation.

One of the elders instructed them to calm down and each sit on one of the many rocks placed in a circle. The elders then asked the men to calmly present their points of view.

Everyone listened as each man explained that his cow was rare. One was red, with a white spot on its neck—a highly prized colouring indeed,

Darius commented in his letter. The other man had a bull that was white, with a moon-shaped black mark near its tail. Both men had travelled far with their bulls. And both men were elders, part of good delegations in their respective communities, and had many sons. They'd been to two graduation ceremonies already.

"What do you think?" Darius' father asked him.

Darius' eyes scanned the wrinkled faces of the elders and then his own father's. He knew his own eyes must have shown bewilderment, for he was truly unsure why the elders would ask him for advice in settling a dispute. He tried to calm his racing thoughts.

"I...I...I," he stuttered. "I think," he started after a brief pause, "that both men deserve, from their past experiences and the greatness of their bulls, to be first," he said. "It would be a blessing to eat the flesh of both these cows."

"But we can only have one for the main ceremony," an elder interjected.

The other men nodded their heads in agreement.

"What would you do?" one of the elders now asked, waving for Darius to continue.

Darius looked up at the sky and thought about the predicament. He closed his eyes tight and asked: "Enkai, give me the answer." After a short time, he spoke.

"It is also a great blessing, perhaps an even greater blessing, for a family's bull to be slaughtered at the ceremony at the very end, is it not?"

The elders and the two men urged him to continue.

"So...what if one man's bull is slaughtered for the first ceremony, to welcome everyone to the graduation and the other man's bull is slaughtered at the end, as a way to congratulate all the warriors for graduating. How does everyone feel about that?" he asked.

"Maybe this is good," one of the men replied.

"Yes, maybe, yes," the other man grunted.

"But how do we choose who goes first and who goes last?" the first man probed.

Darius remembered how he and his friends would draw sticks on the *boma* to choose who went first in a game of tag when they were children. He also thought of school, and how the football referees tossed coins into the air to determine which team was on offence first. He decided on the former for the men who owned the bulls. Darius thought they may never have seen a coin before, and might think it superstitious to choose such an important thing in a Western-style way. "Draw sticks," Darius said confidently. "Whoever draws the longer stick goes first."

Everyone agreed.

The man with the red cow ended up being chosen to go first, while the white cow would be slaughtered for the final day of the ceremony.

That night, Darius went to sleep right where he sat down to drink some cow's blood, on the ground near the cows.

And the next day there was no time to speak with his father, as an elder sent him out with the cows before his *papai's* eyes had even opened. But it seemed as if word of his idea for settling the conflict had spread. Every elder Darius passed would lower his head and nod.

When several moons had passed and the elders kept greeting him in this way, he finally asked his father why he was being treated differently.

"'One day you will be a leader,' isn't that what the *oloiboni* told you?" his father replied. "'One day you will be an important person among the Maasai.'"

Darius had always assumed that the prophet meant that he would be part of one of the delegations, likely the peaceful delegation since his grandfather and father were both members. It would be a great accomplishment, for members of delegations were very well respected in their communities. But Maasai are not boastful, and some elders have been asked to leave delegations if they have shown pride. So Darius knew he had to stay focused on his graduation duties and avoid thinking too much about his future.

For many months, Darius used his time at the graduation site to get to know the other Maasai, who had come from all over Maasailand for the ceremony. In his letters he spoke of how he would walk through the *boma* and meet Maasai speaking dialects of Maa he never heard before, and in some cases found difficult to understand.

He met everyone with a friendly handshake and listened to them tell stories about their lives.

Everyone, in recent times, had been impacted heavily by drought, and now depended on eating beans and rice in addition to cows, milk and blood for their survival. And everyone was grappling with how they handled sending their children to school, while preserving their culture.

Darius spent his nights choral chanting with the other warriors. He also listened to the elders' concerns and their stories about Maasai youth who had left the Mara, some for good, to work in the big cities. "Everyone is facing the same issues," Darius wrote. "Everyone, from the northern reaches of the Mara to the southern."

Chapter 19

My generation: Wilson and the ceremony of a lifetime

Something inside of Darius had changed by the time Jackson and I finally joined up with him for the final part of the Maasai graduation. He was calm, his movements slow and deliberate but strong, like when he moved his hands through the air to animate some speech. He no longer seemed like an enthusiastic high school student or a young, eager Maasai warrior.

He now knew how to listen, his eyes unblinking, nodding, following conversations, how to really listen to others. I felt I could tell him anything, even my fears, such as failing a test at school or speaking to the students at school as a leader—fears a Maasai would never usually confess to another.

Darius' eyes had wrinkles around the corners, too, as if he had become a man in the short period of time since we'd last seen each other.

"You are wise and old," I chided. He patted me on the back and drew me into a long embrace.

But we had no time to catch up.

We all felt it: a knowing. Our great prophet, the *oloiboni*, had arrived at the ceremony, which meant we were close to the end.

Darius' *papai* had left to attend some meetings with the other elders and the prophet. Before he departed, he explained that they were choosing the leader of our generation of Maasai. "As you know," he had said, "the Maasai are divided geographically into nine areas, with one leader being identified for each region. It is a great, great honour for a junior warrior to be chosen as a generation leader."

A few suns later, we were told to get ready for the ceremony that would include the announcement of who would be the leaders of our Maasai generation.

The junior warriors donned all the beaded necklaces, bracelets and belts they had been given since they were children. We dressed in our new red *shuka*s and plaid blankets to indicate we were initiated warriors. We then gathered together in a flat open part of the savannah and waited…and waited…and waited for the elders to come. Some impatient young men from Tanzania broke out in choral chanting.

Haeee! Hoyoo hoooo!
Haeee! Hoyoo hoooo!
Haeee! Hoyoo hoooo!
Purko ai eyieyio munje
Angoru altonet sidai caitotonie
Haeee! Hoyoo hoooo!
Haeee! Hoyoo hoooo!
Haeee! Hoyoo hoooo!
Purko ai eyieyio sidai namirie
Nauteti.

"Shush, shush, shush," waved the elders, when they eventually walked out into the middle of the large circle we had formed.

The crowd quieted, so much so that I could hear the *hadada ibis* calling out as they flew above us. It was a great accomplishment, given that there must have been about a thousand junior warriors there, all of us holding our breath in anticipation.

Beside the elders were nine prophets, each representing one of the Maasai regions.

Two senior elders took turns explaining that the prophets had sat together and decided on the leaders of the generation. These leaders would meet with the elders at least once every full moon cycle, and pass on Maasai wisdom to the warriors in their district, they explained.

The leaders would offer instruction, based on their own and elders' wisdom, in every aspect of Maasai life: how to conduct themselves as husbands and be part of delegations, and how to settle disputes when buying and selling cows at the markets.

"They will be the leaders in helping you navigate your way between Maasai and Western culture," another elder interjected. "They will be your guides. How they conduct and live their lives is how you should live yours."

I looked over at Darius, who was staring at our prophet, Oloruma. Oloruma's eyes in turn, were fixed on Darius.

A shiver ran through me.

I knew.

Darius was the chosen one.

It takes years for our prophets to choose our generation leaders. It is not something we, as children, strive for, either. As junior warriors, we just want to be good Maasai. We know that being a generation leader is a great blessing, but also responsibility. We pray to Enkai, asking that if we are to lead, she give us the strength to do so. And if we are not to be leaders, then we do what we can to support those who are. It is the Maasai way.

As Rotiken has told me, our prophets get an inkling, a premonition almost, when they first meet the child who will come to represent an entire generation of Maasai warriors. Over the years, the prophet keeps an eye on the child.

The elders, who have been told of the *oloiboni's* premonition, watch too. They pay attention to the child, seeing how he settles disputes, masters the Maasai way of living, how he listens and how he is respected among his peers.

One sign of who will become that leader: at the graduation ceremony, they will be given more difficult tasks to perform than the other junior warriors.

So when Oloruma walked away from the elders and headed straight to Darius, I was not surprised.

Oloruma removed Darius' new red plaid blanket and placed a red-dyed cow skin in its place. He then handed Darius a smooth black cane made out of wood from the acacia nilotica (or *olkiloriti* in Maa), which showed others his position within the generation. Oloruma drew some white chalk figures on Darius's face and hair, and made some hand gestures over Darius's head.

The two then looked up to the sky, closing their eyes and letting the rays of Enkai bless the decision.

Once the nine generation leaders were chosen, the crowd of Maasai warriors erupted into cheers, choral singing and leaping. The festivities lasted for four full days.

A few times, we left the celebrations to convene in our regional groups to discuss various names for our generation, and our colours. With the elders' blessings, eventually the generation name *Ilmeshuki* was chosen, which means "those who will not give up."

Our generation of Maasai, an elder announced, was seen as a great generation, one that would bring change to the Maasai, much like another generation called *Ilmeshuki*, about two hundred years earlier, had done. The previous *Ilmeshuki* generation had perfected the raid and the slaying of lions. They taught the Maasai how to live good, fulfilling and honest lives, wanting for little and being respectful of others.

Our generation, our prophet continued, would be about education. Our character traits would be bravery in wisdom and knowledge, not bravery in the raids or against our foes like the lion or the Kipsigis.

The *oloiboni* then prophesied that we, the *Ilmeshuki*, would help heal the Maasai and the world. Our colours would be sky and royal blue, to represent the air that holds up Enkai.

When the *oloiboni* was done, I stood silently, while the other Maasai warriors cheered. I was in a bit of shock. Previously, I had had no idea what kept propelling me to continue with my studies, I just knew that I had to. And somehow, the support came with my conviction. Now, attending the final few weeks of my generation's graduation ceremony, the *oloiboni* confirmed for me what I had felt instinctively my entire life. My education was important not just to me, but to all of the Maasai.

Chapter 20

Vows and vocations: Jackson and the greater world

After our Maasai graduation ceremony, Wilson and I graduated from high school. And we both dreamed of going to college. We wanted to become leaders in our communities: Wilson wanted to be a doctor, and I, a politician.

But we didn't have any money. Our families had sold all the cows we could possibly ask them to sell. And while we talked about asking our *il-papaini*, our fathers, to convene another *harambee* to pay for us to go to college, we decided in the end to take a break from school. Our families and communities had done so much for us that we wanted to give back for a while.

Wilson took a volunteer job as a teacher's assistant in an elementary school in a remote area of the Mara. The school was run down. The roof leaked, the walls had holes in them and the students had to share textbooks and pens. He slept in a small building up the hill from the school, the floor of which was the savannah. He shared this home with two other teachers.

The students of the area had many illnesses and frequently missed school due to malaria, flu, stomach ailments and diarrhea.

Wilson loved being a teacher, but seeing first-hand the suffering of the Maasai children made his heart grow heavy. A feeling began to sink inside of him, like it had in me a few years earlier. The misery around him became his own. He was Maasai and he needed to help make a difference in the quality of these children's lives, in whatever way he could.

I wanted to earn an income, so I asked my father if I could sell two of my cows; I would use the profits to open a small shop in Naikarra Town. Even if I was married and headed a household of my own, I would still have to ask permission of my father to sell my cows, sheep or goats. Until he dies, all that I own is also his.

Luckily, my father said it would be okay.

With my money in hand, I headed to Narok, where I bought large bags of sugar and flour, *shukas* and sandals. I then returned to Naikarra Town and opened my store.

I began earning money, and quickly. Due to the droughts, most Maasai now purchased products at markets, rather than depending solely on their cows for sustenance. I started using all the skills I had learned in high school, not just math in the taking and giving of Kenyan shillings, but even social studies. Naikarra is both a region and a trading town en route to the border of Tanzania, so I was meeting and communicating with Muslims travelling to Ethiopia, Samburu (who many foreigners mistakenly think are also Maasai but they aren't) and Maasai from Tanzania visiting family or attending ceremonies in the Mara.

After the sale of those two initial cows, my father, my brothers and I no longer needed to sell any more of our livestock. Whatever we needed—a new *shuka* for my sister, honey for my mother to make local brew for a ceremony—I was able to provide.

One day, about six months into my business, my young sister Resian got very sick with malaria. She was given the bark of an East African greenheart tree, mixed with *Olea Africana*, which we use to treat the illness, but she didn't get better. Her fever only got worse, and she developed a rash. Her breathing became laboured and my mother and I worried she might not survive.

The hospital was several hours' drive away in Narok. And the medicines that she would likely be prescribed by the doctor were not free.

I carried Resian from our *boma* into town wrapped in a blanket, her face and skin clammy from fever. She talked gibberish, in and out of a state of dreaming, and her eyes were glazed.

My mother held her hand the entire way and prayed.

We arrived at Naikarra Town, our first stop on the way to Narok, as night fell and learned we had missed the last *matatu* for the night. We rested until morning in a small guest house there, wiping Resian's forehead and skin with cold water every time she stirred.

The next morning, we caught the first *matatu*. And when we arrived at the hospital, the doctor saw Resian immediately—she was that ill.

I paid for the medicines Resian needed, and the fees for her to rest in the hospital for the week. I also paid for all of our food for the week—all from my earnings at the shop.

Resian slowly emerged from her delirium and fever. By day seven, the sweet, happy Resian, who always served me *chai* sweetened with honey and warm *chapatti* as soon as I set foot in the *boma* from school, had returned. But she likely wouldn't have survived, the doctor told my mother and me, if we had come to the hospital any later than we did.

One day, not long after Resian was fully recovered and back at the *boma*, I visited Rotiken. Wilson, whom I had not seen in more than ten months, was there with a group of young people from a Canadian non-profit group called Free The Children. His volunteer position at the school had ended and he had taken on his first paying job, as a tour guide.

The young Canadians were camped out in tents, behind Rotiken's hut. They were building a classroom at our old primary school, and sleeping and eating right alongside Rotiken and his family.

Wilson explained to me that Canada was far away and very cold. "In their winters, white flakes like salt fall from the sky. It's called snow," he told me. "And the days are as cold as the river, how it feels first thing in the morning during the coldest days of July."

I shivered at the thought, for our mornings at that time of year were very chilly.

I watched Wilson work with the group for two days. I saw how dedicated the young people from Canada were, making sure the school's cement walls were sturdy and straight and that the roof didn't leak. Maasai children from several *boma*s watched too, wide-eyed and telling me they hoped they could go to school and, if so, that this would be their schoolhouse.

Unlike Wilson and me, who had spent time in Nairobi and with tourists, some of these Maasai children had never seen a white person before.

At one point they grabbed my hand, took me around in behind some bushes and made me watch as they rubbed their skin with ashes they had taken from a firepit, making their faces and arms white.

"We can be white too!" they said, giggling.

I laughed as the children poured the ashes over my head, making me look old, with grey hair, like a wise man.

As they resumed their play, I looked at the ash-covered children and then at the Westerners building the school. Their warm smiles made me feel at ease. I wondered what would compel these young people from North America, who were about the same age as me, to travel all the way to Africa to help people they didn't know. I realized we were connected in a way that we Maasai hadn't experienced much in the past.

The Maasai have always said that if a foreigner takes our photo, they steal our blood. It's just an old wives' tale young people were always told, in order to protect our culture from outsiders.

But now we allow people to take our photos, and we hope others let us take theirs. The Maasai want to reach out to foreigners, but we don't want to lose ourselves in doing so, either. We want a circle, where foreigners come to us, and we come to them.

At the end of my stay with Rotiken, I asked Wilson what he did for the non-profit group. He told me he was teaching the young people about Maasai culture and the importance of preserving the land, and helping the group build schools and set up environmental and social programs in the community, similar to what we did with our clubs at school.

I asked Wilson if I too could work there. He said he would speak to the staff.

Soon after, drought came again to the Mara. I closed up my shop and went back to Tanzania with the cows. While I was there, Jonathon got a phone call saying that Free The Children wanted to meet me, to see if I would do the same job as Wilson. One of my brothers brought Jonathon's message to me.

I left the cows with my brothers and walked back to Kenya, doing what should have been a five-day walk in half the time. I arrived home caked in mud and sand, but enthusiastic and ready to go.

I bathed myself and my clothes in the river and dug the dirt out from underneath my nails. Two days later, I was at my first job interview.

The Free The Children staff told me they needed a Maasai person who could speak English to help the guests learn about our culture, including telling them Maasai stories and how we throw a spear and a *conga*. Mostly, I was told, the groups I would be leading would want to know about my life out on the Mara and what the Maasai, known worldwide as a warrior culture, were really about.

I laughed and raised my left hand. I stretched my fingers to make a peace sign. "This is what the Maasai are about," I said with a smile. "Peace!"

For the next year, I took Western youth on tours of the Maasai Mara and taught them about the Maasai. For a while I was nervous when these strangers would ask me about slaying lions. By this time it was illegal to kill a lion in Kenya, unless the lion was attacking the livestock or a *boma*. The experiences Darius, Wilson and I had at the cave turned out to be among the last that any Maasai warrior has had.

Very few Maasai were heading out to the caves anymore for their rite of passage. They risked being fined if they did.

But before I would tell them about my experience, I would search their eyes for any sign of dishonesty. "Are you police?" I once asked a large man with yellow hair. "Government? Will I get arrested if I tell you?"

After about four groups in, I no longer worried. The young people were very friendly and I found myself just as interested in their culture as they were in mine.

Then, about a year into my work with Free The Children, I learned that Wilson and I would have the chance to see their culture up close, by travelling to Canada and taking part in the organization's country-wide event known as We Day.

I had only ever been to Nairobi and across the Mara to Tanzania. I had never seen an ocean, a pine tree or a grizzly bear. Sometimes, over the Mara, I would see small airplanes soar above me, like big eagles. Now, I would be taking two or perhaps even more airplanes, I was told, and big ones—planes that could seat up to 250 people.

When I told my parents about the airplanes, they stared up into the sky and squinted into the sun. "If we were meant to fly, Enkai would have given us wings!" my *papai* said.

It turned out that Wilson and I had a lot to do before we left. When Free The Children staff went to purchase our plane tickets, they asked us for our passport numbers.

"What is that?" I asked.

"Okay, well, since you have never travelled," said the young woman, "we'll have to get you a passport, which allows you to enter another country. What about your birth certificate? I can at least book the tickets with that."

"What is a birth certificate?" Wilson asked.

The pretty blonde woman, with faded blue eyes like the sky around the sun, tilted her head to the side. "You don't have birth certificates?" she asked, with a bit of surprise in her voice.

Wilson and I shook our heads.

"Hospital records to show where you were born?"

"We were born in our *manyattas*!" I said proudly.

"So no one recorded your date and time of birth?"

"I was born during the night," I replied. "It was a good birth. An auspicious birth."

And so, my life of paperwork began.

To go to Canada, I had to first go to the hospital in Narok and get a birth certificate. The nurse in the reception area eyed Wilson and me suspiciously. "Why do you want to leave this country?" she eventually asked. "Are we not good enough here?"

"No," I exclaimed. "We are just going overseas and then coming right back."

"Do you have any idea how old you are?" she then asked, picking up her pen.

"Fifty," Wilson blurted. "We're both about fifty!"

She put the pen down and stared at us. "You must have some fountain of youth on that *boma* of yours if you are fifty," she said, her lips puckered up in a smirk. "I think you are both about twenty, twenty-three maybe, no more...not fifty."

"Ahh...maybe...maybe..." I said, adding up in my head my years in elementary school and high school.

"Since we don't know your birthdates, we are going to record you simply as January 1...January 1, 1986," she said, writing something down on a piece of paper. Then she took our photographs and sent us to Nairobi to get our passports.

Within a few months we were on our first airplane. The entire time, about fifteen hours in total from Nairobi to a place called Brussels and then to Toronto, Canada, Wilson and I kept our eyes glued to the TV screen in front of us that showed our plane's progress.

At the time, we had no idea what a real TV was, even though we had heard of it before, or that we could watch movies on the airplane. We just kept our eyes glued to the monitor, afraid to sleep in case the airplane crashed.

We also didn't eat. Our stomachs were too upset from our shaking nerves.

When we arrived in Canada, the weather was not cold, like I had thought it would be. And salt was not coming from the sky. It was early October, and I was told that the temperatures would dip soon, but had not yet.

Almost every day, someone from Free The Children would whisper to us that we were going to meet famous celebrities. "Actors on television, singers and even politicians." But Wilson and I didn't know what "famous" and "celebrities" meant. We only knew people as elders or headmasters or our friends.

We also didn't know that Canadians and Americans called football "soccer." We went to a Canadian football game, only to discover the sport was as foreign to us as the women we saw on the streets wearing cow boots that stretched up their legs to their knees. Even the ball was shaped differently, like an egg, not a sphere.

We were in awe, nonetheless, and not because the game was so fast or because we were being greeted by well-known players, including Michael "Pinball" Clemons, who was retired but invited us down to the field to watch the game with him. Wilson and I wondered how the players, including "Pinball," got so big! I'd never seen any Maasai, or anyone else for that matter, with muscles that bulged on their arms and thighs like these men had.

Back at our friend Cameron's place, where we were staying, I suggested to Wilson that these Canadians must drink a lot of cow's blood and milk.

Wilson and I took our very first boat ride on Lake Ontario, and I was shaking in my shoes the entire journey because I do not know how to swim. If I fell overboard, I would be washed away, for sure, just like I thought I would be that night Wilson and I had to traverse the rapids of the overflowing Mara River.

In Toronto, I saw a building taller than any in Nairobi and heard it was called the CN Tower. In British Columbia, Wilson and I took a helicopter ride. We saw snow for the very first time at the top of a mountain named Rainbow. Then I fell while ice skating and split open my chin. Everyone came to my side, touching me and saying I needed help. I pleaded with them to return to their fun. Instead, they took care of me and rushed me to the hospital.

The doctor, with grey hair and black-rimmed glasses, wanted to give me something called anesthetic and a painkiller, before stitching up the wound. I gasped. "Just stitch it up," I said. "I am a Maasai warrior and I do not flinch!"

His eyes popped open and he stood looking at me with a stunned expression. "Okay," he eventually said, as he began fixing my chin. It hurt and I wished I had taken the anesthetic, after all. But I wasn't going to tell him or anyone else that!

I returned to Kenya with bags full of T-shirts, Canadian flags, posters, balls and even a deck of playing cards. I gave everything away except for some books I bought at Grouse Mountain, a wilderness park, where I saw my first grizzly bear and wolves.

What I came to realize during this trip is that when we share our cultures, we enrich each other's lives. It is not about one culture claiming dominance over another. But about being one with each other, and yet separate. The way you want others to respect and learn from you, do the same for them. On the Mara I was showing foreigners my culture. When I visited Canada, they showed me theirs. It was harmony.

Chapter 21

Bright lights, big city:
Wilson, Nairobi and the future

The first time I went to Nairobi, I was in Grade 8. It was an educational field trip; a four-hour bus ride to and from the city in a single day, to view Kenya's parliament buildings and learn more about the country's history. During this field trip, I saw the city's parks and downtown core, which were designed, I was told, by the British to look a little like their big city, London.

I heard all about Kenya's colonization under the British and the slave trade and the Maasai's lack of involvement in both. In fact, the Maasai, I discovered, were one of only a few cultures in the world left intact, similar to generations of old. This surprised me, because the Maasai who live near the game reserve hotels have lost much of their culture. They work as cooks, cleaners and tour guides; they let foreigners take their photos and they eat mostly Western diets of rice, beans and vegetables.

Some of the other Maasai and I were not allowed to go to the washroom by ourselves or wander the streets. "None of you have ever been to the city before," said our social studies teacher. "You may be able to find your way home in the middle of the Mara in the blackness of night. But you'll get lost on these streets of endless cement and tall buildings made of glass."

He was right. I was very afraid in this big city and I remained close to my teacher, so close I sometimes stepped on his heels.

The year before I headed to Canada, I returned to Nairobi to go to university. Jackson came too.

My palms were sweaty as I filled out the paperwork for my courses— botany and tourism—and then was shown the dorm room that Jackson and I would share for the year. I was nervous that I might get lost in this big city, for the campus was located right downtown, not far from the parliament buildings I visited in elementary school. Jackson and I started out by exploring the sprawling gardens of the university.

In the entire university, I was told, there were only six Maasai students, out of a population of about a thousand. One school administrator told Jackson and me that we shouldn't wear our *shukas* and blankets in the city. "Foreigners will stop and ask for your photograph and ask all sorts of questions about your life. The locals, on the other hand, may try to steal your money thinking you don't know much about the city."

"Steal!" I exclaimed, for stealing was as foreign to me as drinking cow's blood is to Westerners…except, of course, when it came to stealing cows.

"Yes, steal," the administrator said matter-of-factly. "Watch your money closely."

Jackson and I both had some money from what we had earned working as tour guides for Free The Children. I wrapped the bills into a tight wad, tied elastic around it and slipped it into a pocket in my pants.

Jackson and I then decided to go shopping.

There were so many cars on the roads, I had to stop and catch my breath from all the fumes choking my lungs. And the cars weren't moving. As I later learned, Nairobi is one of the worst cities in the world for traffic. I could walk much faster than the cars moved. But I was told that the city dwellers like their air-conditioned cars and radios, despite knowing that they could get where they wanted to go much quicker on the backs of motorbikes.

I would peer into the windows of these cars and see men in stiff suits reading magazines, women putting pink paint on their nails and combing their hair, and children singing to the music playing on the radio.

Within a day, I missed my cows, the savannahs, the antelopes, the elephants and the sound of the rooster calling to wake me up.

I wanted to go home.

With money from my job, I bought some papayas and watermelon at the market across the street from the university and some books at the campus bookstore. One of those books was a collection of Shakespeare's plays, and I spent my spare time that entire first term reading and re-reading *Romeo and Juliet*. I wondered to myself, "If I fell in love with a Kipsigis woman, would our families bicker?" Not today, surely. "All the tribes in Kenya get along so well," I told Jackson. "I could marry anyone these days!"

Oh…how these words would very soon come back to haunt me.

Jackson and I both chose to study botany due to our love of nature. We also chose tourism because we wanted to learn more about why the Maasai Mara lacked so many services, despite all the foreigners who came to visit us. Jackson's goal was to understand how it all worked, so that when he eventually went into politics he could bring about change.

Jackson and I were quite surprised that we already knew a great deal of what we were being taught in botany class. We learned, for instance, that our traditional medicines for malaria, cholera and typhoid were actually being used in modern Western medicine. We also discovered that taking trees from lush areas and replanting them in barren areas can help lessen the impact of deforestation and help replenish the land. We also understood more about how some of Kenya's wildlife, including the rhinoceros and lions, came to be on the verge of extinction due to the illegal trade of animals and their parts.

Since I had studied some Christianity, I celebrated Christmas Day in 2007 back in my *boma*, with my *papai*, *nini*, brothers and Rotiken, by slaughtering a goat and drinking cow's blood.

Then, on the night of December 26, Rotiken's mood suddenly turned sour. He saw the stars and his spirits sank.

The Maasai believe the appearance of the sky can be an omen for good times...or bad. When the morning star and evening star (which are actually the planets Mercury and Venus) remain more or less in the same location for the entire night, storms are brewing. When the Maasai see this, they must ask the prophet what he predicts is coming.

In the past, the *oloiboni* has prophesied accurately that another community would attack the Maasai, or that they would lose cows. The *oloiboni* has also predicted famine.

In the dim light of the moon that night, I could see Rotiken's face drain of colour. "Something bad is coming," he told me at that moment.

His eyes were framed in dark circles. "Something very bad is coming," he said over and over again. "I see blood."

On December 27, Kenya erupted in civil war. Tribe turned on tribe. The conflict started in the slum areas of Nairobi, over election results. People disputed who had won and took to the streets, attacking and even killing those who supported their opponents.

Rotiken dug his radio out and we listened to the reports, one after the other. Kenyans were enraged...but unlike when the students in the school became angry, there was no one able to settle the crowds. People were killed in front of their children, women raped, children's bodies dismembered, houses set ablaze. The wealthy and the politicians in Nairobi all left on airplanes and helicopters, leaving the poor to fend for themselves.

Surprisingly, the Kipsigis and the Maasai, rivals historically, were peaceful. For one, we were cheering for the same politician, Raila Odinga, who had visited the Mara during his campaign. It was the first time a presidential candidate ever did. And he promised us schools and jobs for the young. But other tribes, who supported incumbent president Mwai Kibaki, fought against Odinga's supporters in the cities who claimed the election had been rigged.

It was one of the bloodiest events in Kenya's history, and intense for a month, before things slowly dissipated.

There is a saying in Maasai that everything is connected and interconnected. *Taleenoi olngisoilechashur*, we are all one thing. And it is our responsibility as individuals to make sure we live right and treat everyone around us as if they are our brothers or sisters.

At the very tip of our machete, for instance, is a metal pin. From the moment we are given our machetes at about the age of ten, we Maasai are taught that we need to be very careful. The way we make the pockets for our machetes involves tiny pieces of leather bound and re-bound around each other. The Maasai machete itself has a very tiny pin that connects the blades. If it comes loose, the blades fall apart. If we are careless with our machetes or neglect the details to make the pocket perfect, the pin of the machete could fall out and the blades hurt us—or worse, hurt the person walking behind us.

This is how the Maasai are brought up to be in this world. We are told to think about our actions at every moment of our lives. The care we take with our machetes is used as an analogy by Maasai elders, in teaching the young to never do something that will hurt the connection of the whole.

When I listened to the newscasts over those violent few weeks, my heart sank. How did it come to this? *Taleenoi olngisoilechashur*. I knew most of the other tribes, somewhere in their history and folklore, must have had similar visions of the world. Where did they go? How were they lost? *Taleenoi olngisoilechashur*!

When the university finally re-opened a few months later, and Jackson and I made our way back to Nairobi on the *matatu*, we could see the destruction all around us. Displaced persons camps had been established by various United Nations agencies in the suburbs. There was garbage littered everywhere. But that was nothing compared to the horror. People's limbs, even corpses, were still lying on the roads.

All my schooling and my personal life as a Maasai juggling two worlds, my culture and that of the West, has led me to believe one thing with certainty: that the modern history of Africa has always been about our leaders thinking of themselves first, and not the generations to come, whereas we Maasai always think of our generation and the generations to come. We never think of I, but we. We always remember, *taleenoi olngisoilechashur*.

When I saw the destruction around me, my goal became to share my Maasai culture with anyone who was willing to hear our story. I also pledged that I would support Jackson when he finally made his way into politics. And help Darius, so he could help Maasai children with school, while at the same time preserving the beauty and wisdom of Maasai culture.

While our elders are fearful of losing our ways, I believe there are many things the world can learn from the Maasai. Our delegations are an example of how politics can work, and work really well. Our elders are chosen on consistency of their actions, not by popularity. Our communities care for our widows and most vulnerable. We care for our children. We care for our sick. Family is the backbone of the Maasai society.

A photographer visited the Maasai Mara in the fall of 2010 and said to me that he sees the Maasai at a crossroads. One way is modernization and the other way is our traditional lives. But I do not see this as a fork, like he does, where we have to pick one direction over another. Modernization is school, allowing our children to dream and getting rid of practices that stifle our progress, like female genital cutting, polygamy and forced marriage. Modernization is having the Maasai broaden their incomes through farming and jobs—even careers in medicine, teaching and law—so we are not dependent on cows all the time, or dependent on corrupt politicians making decisions for us. But doing this does not mean losing our culture. I say it is about making us better.

Among the Maasai, someone who is the age of your mother is also *your* mother. Someone who is the age of your father is also *your* father. Someone of your generation is always your brother. And your wife is your best friend. That is why we want females to be educated and empowered to make decisions with us. All people are people, and the world should reflect that.

Our African and world leaders complain and complain but they never come up with solutions to end the corruption. I want to come up with ideas the Maasai way: as a team, as a delegation, cooperatively. I want to see a free world where all children have access to schools and education, but also have the respect and love of where they came from and where they want to go.

I finished my year at university more convinced than ever about my future. I would do whatever it took to make sure Maasai children remembered *taleenoi olngisoilechashur*. Any foreign person I would meet, I would tell them about *taleenoi olngisoilechashur*. And any Kenyan whose path I crossed, I would remind them that *taleenoi olngisoilechashur* is about all of us, not the blood that spilled and covered the earth in red on that terrible, terrible December day. But all of us—living in harmony—together.

Epilogue

All of the young men in this book—Wilson, Jackson, Terugee and Darius—work with Free The Children. Jackson and Wilson are both guides, educating Westerners, young and old about Maasai traditions, including how to throw a spear, how to toss a *conga*, which traditional medicines cure different diseases and, of course, about their legends and prophecies. In their Maasai communities, Wilson and Jackson spend a great deal of time speaking to children and youth about the importance of going to school and how they can juggle their Maasai culture and responsibilities with gaining a Western-style education. They also educate anyone who will listen, Western or African, on the environment and its wildlife, and the importance of preservation and conservation.

Jackson's goal is to become a senior elder, and have the respect of his people. He would like to run for office one day and represent the Maasai in Nairobi—the real Maasai, he says, who stand for peace, harmony and justice.

Wilson would like to be a school teacher or a doctor and work among the Maasai, bringing Western knowledge to his people while also preserving Maasai traditions. He too would like to enter politics, but at the local level, to ensure that corruption is stopped, or prevented, at the point where it so often begins. He considers himself an environmental activist and insists that Maasai voices must be heard worldwide on issues related to global warming, and plans to make that happen.

Darius also wants to be a teacher. He currently takes visitors on game safaris in the Maasai Mara, showing off the animals that slept beside him as he grew up under the stars, drifting off to the whispers of the wind blowing across the grasses. He enjoys meeting people from around the world—learning their cultures and traditions, as well as sharing his own.

Terugee is a father to two beautiful children, and lives in a remote part of the Maasai Mara when he is not working with Free The Children. He is helping support a Maasai school in his community, where the students have seen few Westerners.

In the Kenyan winter season of 2011 (which corresponds with the North American summer), Wilson, Terugee, Darius and this book's co-author, Susan McClelland, travelled to meet with the *oloiboni*. The road trip spanned days and their automobile broke down numerous times. Wilson joked that when the *oloiboni* isn't prepared to see someone, he puts obstacles in their way so they don't arrive too quickly. When the dust-covered car finally pulled into the prophet's quiet, sleepy village in a lush part of the Maasai Mara, where the children had never seen a camera before, the *oloiboni* was finally ready.

That visit marked the first time the great prophet had ever prophesied in front of a Westerner. He foretold that it was time for Maasai values to be disseminated worldwide, to be part of the movement of global healing. He told Wilson and Susan specifically that they would bring these messages to the West and, in turn, the West would start to come to him. Today, the *oloiboni* welcomes everyone to visit, so he can share his great knowledge and vision with more people. And with this book, Wilson, Jackson and the others hope that the traditions and values of the Maasai will find a way into the world.

Acknowledgements

We would like to thank the following people who helped make this book possible. Thank you to Meisi Rotiken, Issah Toroge, Darius Rotiken, Craig and Marc Kielburger, Roxanne Joyal, Ryan Bolton, Sean Deasy, Peter Ruhiu, Michelle Hambly, Robin Wiszowaty, Jodie Collins, Santai Kimakeke and Cameron Kennedy. We would also like to thank all of our colleagues, the guides, facilitators and all of the Free The Children and Me to We staff. Finally, we would like to thank all of our friends in both North America and the United Kingdom for visiting our home and welcoming us into theirs. And not to forget a big thank you to Susan McClelland who helped bring our story to the page. Thank you all.

—*Wilson and Jackson*

I owe a debt of gratitude to the Maasai who trusted and invited me into their culture, shared their stories, their history, their future and their present lives. Thank you.

—*Susan McClelland*

About Free The Children

FREE THE CHILDREN
children helping children through education

Free The Children is the world's largest network of children helping children through education, with more than one million youth involved in our innovative education and development programs in 45 countries. Founded in 1995 by international child rights activist Craig Kielburger, we are a charity and educational partner that believes in a world where all young people are free to achieve their fullest potential as agents of change. Our domestic programs educate, engage and empower hundreds of thousands of youth in North America, the UK and around the world. Our international projects have brought over 650 schools and school rooms to youth and provided clean water, health care and sanitation to one million people around the world.

Visit www.freethechildren.com to find out more.

About Me to We

♏ me to we
Better choices for a better world

Me to We is an innovative social enterprise that provides people with better choices for a better world. Through socially conscious and environmentally friendly products and life-changing experiences, Me to We measures the bottom line, not by dollars earned, but by the number of lives we change and the positive social and environmental impact we make. In addition, half of Me to We's net profit is donated to Free The Children and the other half is reinvested to grow the enterprise.

Visit www.metowe.com to find out more.

Bring a speaker to your school

Bring a speaker to your child's school, your parent and educator association or your workplace conferences—and take away all you need to "be the change."

The team at Me to We has travelled the world to discover the most inspirational people with remarkable stories and life experiences. From community activists to social entrepreneurs, our roster of energetic, experienced speakers are leading the Me to We movement: living and working in developing communities, helping businesses achieve social responsibility and inspiring auditoriums of youth and educators to action.

They leave audiences with a desire to take action and make a difference. They'll make you laugh, cry and gain a new perspective on what really matters. Be warned: their passion is contagious!

Visit www.metowe.com/speakers to learn more.

Join us on a trip to Kenya

If you want to really experience another culture and truly see the world, take a Me to We trip. Sure, you could lounge on yet another beach, surrounded by other stressed-out visitors seeing the usual tourist traps. But why not seek out a volunteer travel experience that radically changes your perspective, positively transforming the lives of others?

Our staff live and work in the communities you'll visit, coordinating schoolbuilding and supporting development in participation with local communities. On a Me to We trip, you'll learn leadership skills, experience new cultures and forge truly meaningful connections.

Over 3,000 adventurous people of all ages have chosen to volunteer abroad with us. You'll do incredible things, like build schools and assist on clean water projects. You'll meet exuberant children excited at new possibilities for learning, and be immersed in local communities.

You'll get your hands dirty digging wells and laying foundations. But you'll love it. You'll come home with a sunburn—and the biggest smile you've ever had on your face. And best of all, you'll have memories that last a lifetime.

Visit www.metowe.com/trips to learn more.

READ BOOKS WITH A REAL MESSAGE

Living Me to We
Craig and Marc Kielburger

We all want to make a difference. Now it's easier to lead a life that makes the world a better place every day. With this uniquely Canadian guide to socially conscious living, activists Craig and Marc Kielburger give you the tools for Living Me to We. After 15 years travelling the country and advocating for social justice, Craig and Marc became inspired to compile their practical tips for change in one handy guide.

Everyone's Birthday
Marc Kielburger

A birthday celebration in Thailand changes the course of a young Marc Kielburger's life. Follow a young Marc Kielburger in this true story about discovering the meaning of friendship and the power that one person has to make the difference of a lifetime.

Standing Tall
Spencer West

Navigating life on his hands, Spencer has always lived with purpose. But living in a world where society seems to dictate happiness, Spencer wanted more out of life than just a paycheck and material possessions. He wanted to have an impact, but wasn't always sure how. That was until he had the epiphany that being different was for a reason. This is the candid, coming-of-age story of a young man's journey of working hard, laughing a lot and always standing tall.

The World Needs Your Kid
Craig and Marc Kielburger and Shelley Page

This unique guide to parenting is centered on a simple but profound philosophy that will encourage children to become global citizens. Drawing on life lessons from such remarkable individuals as Jane Goodall, Elie Wiesel and Archbishop Desmond Tutu, award-winning journalist Shelley Page and Craig and Marc Kielburger demonstrate how small actions make huge differences in the life of a child and can ultimately change the world.

Free the Children
Craig Kielburger

This is the story that launched a movement. *Free the Children* recounts 12-year-old Craig Kielburger's remarkable odyssey across South Asia, meeting some of the world's most disadvantaged children, exploring slums and sweatshops and fighting to rescue children from the *chains* of inhumane conditions.

My Maasai Life
Robin Wiszowaty

In her early 20s, Robin Wiszowaty left the ordinary world behind to join a traditional Maasai family. In the sweeping vistas and dusty footpaths of rural Kenya, she embraced a way of life unlike she'd ever known. With full-colour photographs from her adventures, Robin's heart-wrenching story will inspire you to question your own definitions of home, happiness and family.

Me to We
Craig and Marc Kielburger

Me to We is a manual, a manifesto and a movement. It's a philosophy that is both timeless and revolutionary. It's about finding meaning in our lives and our world by reaching out to others—by thinking *we* instead of *me*. In this book, Craig and Marc Kielburger share the knowledge they have gained through living lives of service. Their own reflections and ideas are complimented and reinforced by contributors like Richard Gere, Dr. Jane Goodall, Kim Phuc, Her Majesty Queen Noor, Arch Bishop Desmond Tutu and Oprah Winfrey.

Global Voices, The Compilation: Vol. 1
Craig and Marc Kielburger

Global Voices aims to tell the untold stories of people and issues from around the world. With a foreword from Archbishop Desmond Tutu and discussion questions to help spark debate, this book will inspire young readers to deepen their understanding of issues and explore how they can change these headlines. Tied together from Craig and Marc's columns that have appeared in newspapers across Canada, *Global Voices* touches on the tough issues in an enlightening, enjoyable read.

Lessons from a Street Kid
Craig Kielburger

After starting Free The Children when he was 12-years-old, Craig Kielburger continued his crusade in Brazil. It was on the streets of Salvador, Brazil that Craig learned first-hand the stories of street children. In this easy-to-read, full-colour illustrated children's book, the reader learns about the joys of these very children. Follow the adventure perfect for young readers that defies borders in the universal act of generosity.

My Maasai Life: A Child's Adventure in Kenya
Robin Wiszowaty

Follow a young Robin Wiszowaty as she travels to Kenya for the first time. Living with the Maasai people, Robin explores the land with her new family. Getting water, finding wood and singing songs. And don't forget the zebras, cows and giraffes. It is all a part of the adventure with the Maasai. With Robin as a guide, the full-colour illustrations only enhance any child's own adventure into the world of the Maasai.

Visit www.metowe.com/books to see our full list of bestselling books.

The Buy a Book, Give a Book promise ensures that
for every Me to We book purchased, a notebook will
be given to a child in a developing country.

STAY UP-TO-DATE WITH WILSON AND JACKSON
AND ME TO WE

twitter.com/realmetowe   facebook.com/metowe

Go to **www.metowe.com** to start living *me to we*.